A M

what grows in

the space it

left behind

H. SAINT JAMES

What Grows in the Space It Left behind
Copyright © 2022 by H. Saint James

tellwell

Tellwell Talent
www.tellwell.ca

ISBN
978 0-2288-6429-5 (Hardcover)
978-0-2288-6428-8 (Paperback)
978-0-2288-6430-1 (eBook)

To you.

To the person that you have been.
And to the one that you will become.

James

"Please don't leave," I said frantically, but quietly.

Too quietly.

I held his arms, desperately, looking to him for any kind of sign that he might be reconsidering.

All the things I couldn't say rushing to my mind.

Don't leave me like this.

Don't leave me here.

I'm scared.

I can't do this on my own.

He looked at me, the empathy draining from his face.

"You can't even cry… watching me leave and you can't even fuckin cry."

His voice was cold, irritated.

The harsh shift in the way he looked at me now made me realize he was serious. He was leaving.

All the traces of love I used to feel from those eyes were gone, like a light had gone out.

Slowly… and then all at once.

Isn't it funny how that can happen sometimes?

One day you think you're looking at the love of your life and the next you're suddenly strangers.

Familiar strangers.

And I didn't blame him.

He must have been exhausted of me, even now.

I had asked so much of him over the last year, and after all of this I couldn't even give him the decency of tears.

The signal that I was, in fact, sad and that I did really want him to stay.

But he was right… I couldn't cry.

I don't think I knew how to in moments like that.

He jerked his arms from my grasp, spinning around to grab his bag, which had been filled hastily with a small fragment of his belongings moments before.

I stepped backwards slowly, moving away from him.

The space between us suddenly felt like miles, even inside this tiny apartment.

He turned back around, brushing passed me without meeting my gaze as he made his way towards the door.

The large, heavy blue door that looked more like something you would see from the inside of an old asylum than a downtown apartment.

Heavy and awkward.

One you have to pull with so much force it made you question even bothering to leave.

I watched his hand reach out to take the handle, as he pulled, effortlessly, making his way out into the night.

The door slammed hard on its way back to its frame, and I was engulfed immediately into the realization that I was alone.

Really alone.

The sudden silence was only touched by the soft hum of the cars passing outside our apartment window.

Or was it just my apartment window now?

My mind began to race with all the thoughts I had been avoiding.

Where is he going?

What am I am supposed to do now?

Why doesn't he love me?

… why doesn't he love me?

And then I felt it.

The knot in my stomach began to unravel and tears slowly began to build behind my eyes.

My hands started to shake.

I tried to reach out to something around me to steady myself, but there was nothing.

My knees buckled as I dropped to the floor, the weight of the last few months, few years, pushing me down, relentlessly.

I was exhausted.

My hands pressed into the cold laminate in front of me, trying to steady myself enough to get back up, but the energy wouldn't come.

And just like that, the cold floor in front of me reminded me of something else. Something I was always trying to forget.

But you can't forget those kinds of things.

Not when something as simple as the floorboards makes you remember.

The memory of that night came flooding in, the way it did... the way it always did.

Not now, I thought to myself.

I don't want to think about it now.

But that's the thing about memories... you don't always get to choose when they come back.

"Please stop," I whispered quietly, bargaining with myself to release me from the images that were gathering inside my mind, pushing their way forward.

My voice finally cracked, allowing the carefully held tears to make their way down my cheeks.

I could never seem to get far enough away from those memories.

The way the lights had flickered on the ceiling.

The way the cold tiles felt on the floor.

The blood.

I tried to take a deep breath in, but it wouldn't come.

My lungs refusing to fill in cruel defiance.

And is this what my life had come to?

A moment in time that I could never undo.

A memory I was forever trying to escape.

Maybe.

I felt like I was constantly numb.

Walking around outside of my body, watching my life unfold and unravel in waves, but never being able to reach out and touch anything… control anything, command anything.

But every night and every morning and throughout the day my mind replayed the same things.

Over and over.

The tiles.

The blood.

His voice.

Flashbacks, I had heard someone call them.

Every cell in my being was screaming to be released from this torture, only to wake up another day and do it all over again.

And I was sober now.

What a joke.

It was too much.

And it had gone on for too long.

As I sat there, wiping the tears from my face one by one, I noticed a small white pocket knife that lay innocently in front of me, just within arm's reach.

It was oddly out of place.

I knew every corner of this apartment and more specifically where each of our belongings sat.

I was meticulous about it.

The knife stood out.

My name was engraved on the back of it. A gift from my father on one summer day in Switzerland.

I wondered how it had gotten there. Perfectly parallel to my frail figure.

My heart sank.

I wanted so badly to be able to call my family.

But this thought passed through my mind quickly as I realized the timing of this discovery may have very well been fate.

Because everything happens for a reason, doesn't it?

Before I could properly instruct myself on what to do next, I watched, suddenly outside of myself, as my hand reached for the knife, barely able to see what I was doing through the flood of tears.

I opened up the pocket knife quickly, revealing its dull metal edge.

My hands vibrating fiercely, fumbling with this decision.

Do it, I heard her say.

Almost as if she was sitting right next to me, rather than being locked inside my mind.

My inner voice was demanding.

Relentless.

She would speak to me at random and mostly inopportune times.

There were times when she was sweet and soft, and there were times when she was callous and cruel.

But I guess that meant I was cruel.

To myself.

I tried to choke back another wave of tears.

Didn't I at least want myself to live?

Couldn't I, at the very least, bargain with my own inner self?

I closed my eyes tightly, trying desperately to hold back the tears, when I heard her speak to me again.

You're a silly girl... look at what you've become... nothing.

Wasting away in your shitty apartment.

Your shitty life.

Aren't you tired of this?

this...

prison?

I was.

I lifted my right arm up slightly, holding the little pocket knife in my left hand, and without any further hesitation I closed my eyes again and brought my left hand down with such force, connecting boldly to my right wrist in one fast and fluid motion.

It was quick.

Deliberate.

Everything went quiet.

My ears began to ring.

I opened my eyes.

The tears had stopped.

My heartbeat settling immediately to a slow and methodic beat.

A normal pulse, maybe.

I heard something drop to the floor beside me.

I looked over to see that I had let go of the little white pocket knife, although I hadn't felt myself release it.

A sudden and welcome feeling of euphoria started to drift over me.

Not like the highs I had experienced in the years before.

Better.

Calmer.

Everything seemed to be occurring in slow motion.

Your thigh.

She's still here.

I'm still here.

Your thigh is wet.

The voice in my head felt very far away now. Like when you get out of a pool and your ears are momentarily plugged; coming to the surface for air and being greeted by an odd sensation that every sound around you is somehow muffled.

She became louder.

Closer.

What have you done?

I looked down to my thigh. The one she was so worried about.

My dark blue jeans were beginning to turn black, a small pool of liquid was gathering at the top of my right thigh and slowly drifting towards my knee, expanding in diameter as it travelled.

Blood.

I looked to my wrist, which rested carefully on that same thigh. A large open wound, blood pouring in perfect synchronization with my now increasing heartbeat.

WHAT THE FUCK DID YOU DO?

Suddenly everything around me came into clear, brilliant and immediate focus. Like every light in the city had been turned on and the volume of every sound around me was increasing. My mind, which felt like it had been hovering above my body, shot itself back down to me, colliding and connecting to what had just happened.

What I had done.

Fuck

The shaking in my hands returned, only this time it started in my stomach and quickly made its way through my shoulders, all the way out to my fingertips.

I didn't want to die here.

In that moment it was much more of a decision than a simple thought.

I made a mistake.

I didn't want to die this way.

Not here.

Not anymore.

Fuck.

FUCK.

I stood up quickly, too quickly, trying to remember where I had put my phone.

I needed to call someone.

Yeah, a fuckin ambulance.

I stepped towards the kitchen. Maybe it was in there?

I took three steps forward before my legs protested aggressively, buckling, bringing me back down to the floor.

Keep going.

Oh, now you're on my side? I retorted back to myself, my body growing weak with every new thought that entered.

FUCKIN MOVE, WE'RE RUNNING OUT OF TIME.

I didn't argue. She might be right this time.

I began crawling towards the kitchen, clutching my wrist to my chest. Maybe if I could stop the bleeding, or slow it down I'll have enough time.

As I pulled myself across the divide between the laminate and onto the kitchen floor, I spotted my cell phone sitting on the counter-top.

I knew I wouldn't be able to brace myself from the floor with my damaged wrist, so I quickly held my upper body in position, supported by my left hand pressing against the floor, while I reached my right arm up to grab the phone. As I did, a wave of dark red blood spilled out of the wound, running frantically down my arm towards my neck. I quickly brought my arm down to transfer the phone to my left hand as I clutched my wrist back to my chest.

Sit up.

I can't, I pleaded with her.

It hurts. Everything hurts.

I thought about what I needed to do next.

What number was it again?

What number did I need to dial?

I tried to take a breath in to steady myself, to focus, but I was losing energy.

The force I had exuded in the mere ten feet I had pulled myself through was debilitating.

SIT UP!

She was relentless.

911, I remembered suddenly.

I pulled the phone in front of me and dialed quickly, holding it to my ear, balancing myself as I pressed my elbow to the floor.

I was connected immediately with a calm and assertive voice on the other end.

A woman.

"911. Police, fire or ambulance?"

I paused.

I suddenly didn't know what to say.

Knowing that I was now connected to another human being.

A person.

A person who was alive and whose job it was to ensure I could also be that.

Alive.

She repeated herself, this time more firmly.

"I made a mistake," I began.

This was true. I had made a mistake.

"I think I need an ambulance," I admitted, choking back the tears that were now threatening to flow once more.

I hated asking for help.

And what a cruel joke it was that as I lay on my kitchen floor, bleeding to death, I still struggled with admitting there was a problem.

Was I crazy?

Had I finally gone completely insane?

Yes.

"You need to put pressure on the wound," she instructed firmly, loudly, bringing me back to the conversation, as if she knew I had checked out moments before.

The sleeve of my sweater was covered in blood, and I knew I would need to find something else, quickly, to stop the bleeding.

I looked back towards the simple square space behind me, to the bed that sat in the left corner of the room. There was a towel hanging neatly on the side of the bed. Maybe he had forgotten to pack it.

Go to it.

She was confident in my ability, although my body recoiled at the thought of moving again.

I was exhausted.

GO TO IT.

I pushed myself forward, carefully cradling the phone, crawling again, towards the bed, both of my elbows threating to release themselves of this responsibility.

I reached out to the edge of the bed and pulled myself up to a sitting position, resting my back on the side of the mattress. I grabbed the towel and pressed it against my wrist.

"Paramedics are on their way, stay with me." I had forgotten that she was still there. Her voice was a bit softer now.

I could hear the sirens in the distance, rapidly growing louder.

Breathe in. Breathe out.

Okay.

I tried to keep my body as still as possible.

I felt calmer.

Quieter.

That feeling of euphoria from moments before was returning.

I could sleep, I thought to myself as I struggled to keep my eyes open, the phone slipping from my grip.

My shoulders dropped.

It may as well have been fifty pounds being lifted from them.

Please let me sleep.

The heavy blue door opened suddenly. I could hear a hoard
of footsteps entering my apartment. Heavy footed individuals
dressed in uniform began to surround me, others branching out
into other areas of my little home.

Investigating.

Surveying the damage.

"Keep pressure on it."

A woman in a dark blue uniform knelt in front of me, quickly
securing a tube around my face and into my nose.

Oxygen.

It was cold.

I was cold.

As she did this, I noticed my grip on the towel had loosened. I
was no longer holding it in place.

I was too tired.

It was heavy.

"Keep pressure on it!" she yelled, as she motioned for her
partner to come and assist her.

"Can you tell me what day it is?"

I looked at her blankly.... What day was it?

"Can you tell me what year it is?" She said, maybe hoping that
would be an easier question for me.

"I don't... I don't know."

I heard my voice come to the surface like a whisper.

I just wanted to sleep.

"Open your eyes!" another voice. A man's voice.

I turned my head to see who had joined us on the floor.

A male paramedic leaned into me, adjusting the oxygen tubes.

I felt a sudden burst of icy air enter my airwaves, floating
urgently through my nose, down my throat and into my chest.

I tried to study his face in an attempt to keep my eyes open, as instructed. To remain focused on something, but I was interrupted by the haze of shadowy figures that appeared behind him. I looked beyond him for a moment and realized how many people were crammed into the apartment.

Five, maybe six.

A police officer was standing near the doorway, appearing to summon another person inside.

Dillon.

He came back.

I watched his face carefully as he walked into the apartment.

His jaw dropped as his eyes studied the trail of blood across the living room floor. He raised both of his hands up to the top of his head and began running them through his hair very slowly.

A look of horror and confusion emerging on his face.

I'm so sorry.

I tried to say it out loud but my mouth wouldn't open.

My body finally surrendering to the fatigue.

The police officer ushered him into the kitchen, away from me.

I knew they would be interrogating him.

Two poor kids living in a run-down building in the shit end of downtown.

They always assume the worst when you're poor.

I wanted to call out to him.

I wanted to tell the officer to leave him alone.

It wasn't his fault.

Maybe if they look at your record they'll understand.

She had a point.

Although they didn't help you then either, did they?

Another good point.

I turned my head back to face the female paramedic who was still sitting with me, holding the towel firmly to my wrist. I heard the stretcher being brought inside.

"You're doing great," she said quietly, trying to offer some sort of comfort.

I'm really not though.

I'm really

really

not.

dive down deep into yourself and pull
pull your regrets, your rage, your frightened ambitions
your love, your trust, your damaged submission
and place them ever so nicely along the shore
i will come for you
in waves
and when i do
you will know
for the very weight of everything i have felt
you will feel too
for the pain and the love and light
that you've lost
i will give it back to you.

— *water*

two years earlier

"Why don't you just go back home?"

I looked up to see who was speaking.

A girl I had seen around school before. She seemed nice, but she really didn't know me well enough to be asking a question like that.

I studied her face for a moment, watching her take a long drag off a cigarette. Waiting for me to speak. To give some details.

Tell her fuck off.

"It's not really possible right now," I said casually, turning my gaze from her as I began searching through my bag, pretending to look for something.

I hoped my lack of attention would force her to change the subject or talk to someone else.

The smoking section at school always filled up quickly during this time of day. The short breaks we would get in between classes offering this frantic, momentary reconnection between friends.

"Well, I'm sure your parents would want to have you back home," she continued.

It's not any of your fuckin business though, is it?

I tried to calm my inner voice for a moment, taking a quick breath in before turning back to her. Irritated.

"Yeah. They probably would," I said quickly, as I stood up, swinging my bag over my shoulder, looking around for someone else to talk to.

Someone to steal me from this conversation.

I spotted a friend from my history class sauntering slowly out of the school, making his way over to us. We locked eyes and I waved, smiling, signalling for him to come over.

This seemed to be enough.

The girl turned her back to me to begin talking to someone else that had joined her. Maybe taking my awkwardness as a sign that she had said too much.

And she had.

The entire school may be well aware that I wasn't living at home anymore, but I didn't want to think about that right now.

"Haven't seen you all week!" he exclaimed loudly, smiling from ear to ear as he wrapped his arms around me, embracing me tightly, obviously happy with my return to school today. I had been missing more and more classes recently.

"Did you study for the anthro test?" he asked, as we walked over to a nearby seating area, arms locked together affectionately.

Oh shit.

"Oh god, that's today?!" I asked, as we sat down. I suddenly remembered I hadn't brought the right books with me.

"Yeah," he laughed, pulling out a pack of cigarettes from the front pocket of his shirt.

He pulled two out, offering one to me as we both watched the hoard of other teenagers gathering around us. All immersed in their own conversations, yelling and laughing, enjoying this burst of freedom from the mundane high school classrooms.

"It's okay, I didn't really study either," he said supportively, slowly unlocking our arms as he moved to swipe a strand of my hair away from my eyes.

"You should skip third period with me later. Everyone's going to Danny's."

Danny's would be fun, I thought to myself.

I had been there many times and always felt welcome by his family, specifically his mum.

I wasn't sure if his mother had any real idea what we were up to on the nights we spent there. She worked late most nights. Too late be able to take notice of our adventures, but every time she was there she would always hug each of us and ask how we were doing. Genuinely interested. This crazy band of misfit teenagers constantly invading her house. I wondered if she secretly liked having us there sometimes.

"Yeah let's do that," I smiled, leaning my head against his shoulder.

In that moment I was grateful for him.

Grateful for our group.

Many of us were the same... estranged from family, trying to figure out what to do next.

Every day.

That's probably why we tried to stay close to one another.

It was hard being young.

You try to navigate what it means to grow up while also not being able to see a full month or year in front of yourself.

It confused me when people asked what I wanted to do when I "grow up."

A writer, I would say, or just someone living in an old Westphalia van, travelling along the coast of California. I had never been there, but it seemed like the kind of place you go to find yourself.

"But how will you make money?" They would always ask.

And I never really thought that far ahead.

It didn't feel like I could.

When you spend these years simply trying to survive, the thought of any kind of adult life seems like wasted energy.

Why think about the future when I'm not sure how I'll get through today, or tomorrow?

Maybe that's why teenagers are called reckless.

If your future might not exist, then be wild now.

Will we just wake up one day and be adults?

Suddenly captivated by bursts of knowledge and curiosity?

Making reasonable decisions and settling into life as reasonable people?

Maybe.

But what happens in between now and then?

How do we become... something... or someone?

I didn't have the answer to that yet, but sometimes I felt like I should.

Pretty soon I would be seventeen.

And that alone felt like it was a million years away.

But for now, for today, we would sit together, leaning into one another, appreciating the moment and the time for what it was.

And we wouldn't think about next week, next month or next year.

We would simply think about today.

As far as third period.

And I knew that when we left here later and made our way over to Danny's, there would be a large group of us huddling together, laughing, joking, sharing obnoxious stories about past weeks.

And we would be okay.

And maybe these wouldn't be the people I would still love and care for when I got older.

Maybe that's why I clung to it so much.... There was something inside of me that was desperate to create my own close circle.

My own little family of friends. People I could know and
they could know me and somehow our lives would become
intertwined with familiarities.

I wanted that more than anything.

And I guess sometimes when you want something, you don't
always look at the places you are going to find it.

The very thing or feeling you want becomes an idea you chase.

And sometimes I wondered if I clung to it too much.

you are restless and wild
and they will call it crazy
but when you are quiet and soft
they will call it sad
and when you hear the noises and the voices
i hope you ask yourself
whose am i listening to?
and when you hear the answer
i hope it tells you
you were always wild
and wild you must always stay

— 11

The streets were loud and exciting leading into the park.

I didn't come here often.

At this time of night it was reserved for certain kids.

The cooler kids.

I knew that; we all knew that.

The ones you see in the school hallways, who don't speak to you, but they exude a certain charm and ease of motion in their day.

I didn't really understand it.

I always seemed to feel this overwhelming sense of anxiety.

Panic.

Like I couldn't breathe.

Always.

That made it difficult to talk to people without feeling like I was being too much. Or too little.

Or just not right.

It's exhausting thinking about yourself that much.

But this night was different.

It was the end of July and everyone was drunk with excitement and liquor, knowing that we still had an entire month of summer break left.

There was more to explore, more to experience.

And tonight, the cool kids weren't at the park.

It had been months since I had been home, and the weight of that lifted from my chest as I sat down on the grass, joining a growing group of friends.

Let's not think about that, I thought to myself.

For now.... I can just be here.

And be happy.

I eased into the conversations around me, laughing, smoking, sharing drinks.

It felt good to be drunk.

Very good.

The energy that surrounded us was light and joyful as each of us passed around bottles of liquor, ignoring the disapproving gazes from certain neighbours who peered into the park from their bordering backyards.

The darkness of night came to us quickly, and we knew it was only a matter of time before one of these friendly neighbours decided to call the cops.

I don't really blame them, I thought as I watched a large pile of papers being lit on fire in the centre of the park, feral teenagers dancing around the small flames. Schoolwork.

We were lighting our homework on fire.

I stood up, planning to walk towards the tiny flames that were threatening to grow taller but stumbled clumsily. A girlfriend swooped in behind me, wrapping her arm around my waist, both of us laughing hysterically at the state around us.

And the state of us.

It was one of those moments that you wish you could take in your hands and hold onto. I hadn't felt relief like this in a while.

11:42 p.m.

He took my hand, holding it tighter than I had felt before from anyone else. We were far away from the park now. My girlfriends watching me leave our group, almost like a betrayal, to join this reckless group of boys; and reckless they were. We all were.

What is the point of this youth if we cannot be a bit reckless at times?

And he was cute.

I didn't expect him to want to spend that kind of time with me.

We weren't exactly friends, but we weren't enemies either.

A neutrality between us that seemed to disappear after a few drinks.

The way it does.

We were flirting and kissing and we were alive.

I was happy.

I wondered if, after tonight, the way we talked to each other would change.

I wondered if some social barrier would be broken, and I even wondered if he was going to try and ask me to date him.

I liked the thought of being something to someone.

We were drunk and laughing as we walked down the barley lit path, miles ahead or behind the rest of the group, I don't know which.

And neither of us seemed to care.

He stopped quickly, pulling me back towards him.

"You're really... really pretty," he said, in almost a whisper, seemingly focused.

I laughed, embarrassed, breaking eye contact as I looked at our hands intertwined.

For a moment I wondered if he said that to all the girls he kissed, or was it just me?

Maybe it could just be me... couldn't it?

"You know... we could do... that... I'll be gentle." He grinned.

I knew what he was talking about.

I swayed closer to him, trying to hide my obvious anxiety.

Our eyes met and we both stood still... very still... for a moment.

"I'm a virgin," I whispered.

I wasn't sure if I had said that out loud before.

Maybe I had, but I hated admitting it to anyone.

I had most certainly lied about that fact to boys before.

But something about him, about us and that night, made me want to be honest about it.

Maybe I could trust him.

"I'm nervous," I continued quietly.

He pulled me into him, kissing me with a certain amount of desperation I almost mistook for passion.

And I would have believed it was just that.... Passion.

"I don't want to," I said, surprised by my own honesty as I gently pulled away from his grasp.

"Just think about it," he said, pulling me back to him immediately, grinning with expectation.

The path ahead was difficult to see at this time in the night.

I wondered if our friends would know we came this way.

Or were they ahead of us by now?

Off in the distance was a coffee shop we all knew well.

The only one around here that stayed open twenty-four hours.

I sighed audibly, allowing the last few bits of stress to fall from my shoulders.

I felt his hand tighten around mine as he stepped forward onto the path, gently pulling me to join him.

We made our way into the darkness.

1:47 a.m.

The tiles were colder than I thought they would be.

Tiles.

Floor.

Cold.

Lights.

I heard that if you name the things around you, it can help to stop a panic attack.

Was this a panic attack?

Why can't I breathe?

My hands were shaking violently as I slumped down to the floor.

And then I felt it.

The shaking continuing throughout my body, through my chest, down to my legs.

My shorts were on the floor.

But he was standing with one foot on the edge of them.

Put them back on, my inner voice instructed.

I reached forward and picked up my clothing, tugging it gently away from him just as he began to open the stall door.

It was a small space.

One that seemed much to small, especially now.

Shorts.

Door.

Blood.

Why is there blood?

I looked down at myself. My legs, my ankles… and then to the floor.

Small trails of it everywhere.

I felt sick.

"The best part about this…," he began, turning to look down at me, his voice was cold and lacking any bit of real human emotion, "…is that no one else is gonna know."

I stared at him as he turned his back to me.

The words poured from his mouth.

Delicate.

Violent.

How could something said so quietly seem so loud?

Watching him leave, I opened my mouth to say something, anything, but as I did, I felt the tears begin to build.

I said I didn't want to.

But I was quiet.

I was so quiet.

I was too quiet.

I heard the door swing shut, signalling that I was, in fact, alone.

Don't you fuckin cry.

Get up.

Get up.

Get up.

GET UP.

I pulled my shorts back on, trying frantically to wipe the blood from my legs.

I paused for a moment, pushing my hand onto the tiles beside me for support.

The blood.

It was everywhere.

You're gonna go out there and you're gonna go home.

I didn't understand where these movements and motions were coming from.

My mind seemed to be slowly floating back to me, connecting to my reality as my hands began their own set of movements, piecing me back together.

I wasn't present in my body anymore.

Get up.

Get out of here.

I stood up slowly, pushing my hand into the wall beside me to steady myself.

It seemed like only moments ago I was almost drunk, but now I felt completely sober.

The lights flickering along the ceiling seemed brighter now.

I felt like they were screaming at me.

Open the door, she instructed.

I slowly opened the bathroom door and made my way towards a second door that would lead me back into the café, and then one more door to go to get out of here.

Two more doors.

There was something about the way her voice felt inside of me that night that made me realize she wasn't being condescending in that moment.

She knew I needed the direction.

Step by step.

She knew I wasn't there anymore.

Like a piece of myself had detached.

The piece that's connected to my soul.

Floating up into those flickering bathroom lights.

I pushed myself through the second door.

And then the third.

My knees threatened to buckle with each step.

As I stepped back out into the night, the air seemed much cooler than it had been a few hours before.

I stood frozen for a moment.

My body suddenly wasn't responding to my instructions to keep walking.

I felt dizzy.

I perched myself down on the sidewalk, shivering, trying to understand what had just happened.

I heard an echo of voices in the distance.

I looked out into the darkness that surrounded me now and spotted two shadowy figures with their backs to me as they walked away from the café.

As he walked away.

I couldn't quite make out who he was with, but I could hear the echo of laughter.

Laughter.

He was laughing.

I pulled my knees closer to my chest, watching them disappear into the night.

Out of the darkness I heard a voice say my name, softly, warmly.

I turned to see who was speaking.

"Can I walk you home?"

It was one of the other boys who had been at the park earlier.

I looked past him to see a few more of them. Everyone slowly starting to gather outside the café.

Or had they been here the whole time?

"It's late… you shouldn't walk alone."

This boy.

He was the unassuming type.

A gentle, quiet, awkward boy.

I had had pizza with him one afternoon a few weeks ago, and I remembered him telling me that he didn't like eating in front of girls.

It made him nervous.

I had continued to watch his face turn seven shades of red as he tried his best to finish a slice of pepperoni slathered in hot sauce.

I didn't eat anything, as I sat, trying to hide my obvious grin.

I thought it rather sweet of him to admit that to me that day.

As I watched him looking at me now, I wondered if it would be okay if he walked me home.

The only home I knew of right now.

I looked down to my legs again, suddenly feeling the sensation of something tracing its way down the inside of my thigh.

Blood.

You're still bleeding.

I looked back to him, surveying the genuinely concerned look he had on his face.

I nodded.

We walked for about twenty minutes and I couldn't tell you a thing he said to me during that time, but he talked the whole way.

He didn't seem to be bothered by my silence either.

We approached the little house that I was staying in, and he waited for me to walk up the pathway and open the door before continuing on his way.

I don't know if he actually lived anywhere close to that little house, but I think that sometimes the universe places people in our paths for a reason.

I've never forgotten that walk.

And if you're reading this, thank you.

I pressed on the door as quietly as I could, not wanting to wake anyone.

I knew if I could just make it to the basement, and to the couch, I could lay there. And maybe I could fall asleep.

I was so tired.

I walked carefully down the stairs and into the basement, moving towards my little piece of home.

The loveseat I had been living on for the last several months.

I heard her tossing and turning from the mattress on the other side of the room. It was more than tossing and turning though.

She was awake.

"Where have you been?" she asked, genuinely curious.

I thought for a moment about what to say.

It seemed like my mind still didn't understand what had happened.

I didn't want that to happen.

I said no.

But then you said nothing.

She was right…. At a certain point my voice had left me.

How useless it really is when the other person is stronger than you.

"I think I just lost my virginity," I said quietly, blankly.

I didn't know how else to word what had just happened.

"To who?!" her voice heightened.

My voiced cracked as I said his name.

Each letter slid slowly off my tongue, like a snake.

"Haha, that's so funny," she laughed, mid yawn, too tired to offer any more enthusiasm or enquire further.

I heard her turn over, releasing herself from our brief conversation to return to her sleep.

I desperately wanted to say more.

I wanted to tell her what happened.

To try and piece it together.

Maybe if I could say it out loud, I would understand it.

Maybe he didn't mean to do that.

Maybe he didn't hear me.

Maybe.

I lay down on the little loveseat, pulling a blanket over me, welcoming the warmth.

I should get changed, I thought.

But I didn't.

I couldn't.

I didn't want to touch my own body.

I didn't even know if I was still bleeding.

I pulled my knees to my chest and clung to them tightly.

The tears began to form again, lifting themselves to my eyes, demanding I let them out.

But I couldn't.

there will be a darkness
that will consume every corner of your mind
occupy every room in your soul
it will come for you at the strangest of times
as you laugh whole heartedly amongst those you love
as you sit in celebration or quiet preoccupation
your ears will burn with the sound of its voice
your eyes alive with the sadness of its face
and as you descend into the corridors of your memories
spiralling silently into darkness
look for me there

— don't fall asleep

One Week Later

"Hey!" Ray raced towards me, embracing me affectionately, the way she always did.

It didn't seem to matter if we had been apart for ten days or ten minutes, she was always so excited with our reunion.

And so was I.

I held her close to me for a long time, squeezing gently as she moved her head to kiss my cheek.

"I missed you, Bebe." Her pet name for me. Bebe.

You couldn't help but be happy around Ray.

Without saying anything, I reached into my bag and pulled out a tattered pack of cigarettes.

This was a big deal when one of us had good cigarettes.

"Ahhh!" she exclaimed excitedly, embracing me again.

It felt good to be hugged by her.

We walked up the old familiar path, catching up about our few days apart.

Ray told me all about the new job she had gotten at the grocery store.

"The boss is a real prick, but I made two hundred dollars this week!" she said excitedly, as we sat down together on a nearby bench.

I pulled out two cigarettes.

Perfectly clean, straight, king size cigarettes.

And since the rest of the group wasn't here yet, we could each have our own.

I held them for a moment, cradling them carefully, wondering what I would need to do tomorrow to buy another pack.

I quickly brushed that thought away from my mind, handing one to Ray.

I lit mine, inhaling deeply.

Maybe it wasn't the smoking I particularly liked, but the feeling of taking a full, deep breath.

My chest filling and relaxing methodically.

Something that took a certain amount of effort and concentration for me to do.

I often caught myself holding my breath.

"I heard you uh… had an interesting night last week."

My heart sank immediately.

I wished she hadn't said that.

I wished we could just keep talking about her new job, or her boyfriend, or how we hadn't seen our parents in so long.

Something.

Anything else.

I don't know why I had thought people wouldn't be talking about it.

There had been so many other people who had seen us together that night.

I suddenly flashed back to the image of him walking away from the café.

The laughter.

I could hear it still.

I noticed my hand begin to shake gently.

I gripped the cigarette tighter.

Surely I could tell her.

She was my best friend.

I pushed my back into the bench, looking out to the treeline in front of us, allowing myself to be still for a moment. To think about how I would say this to her. A part of me wanted to blurt it out, the way I usually did with any kind of new information, but another part of me felt like that's not what you're supposed to do with something like this. But how else do you say it? I was so used to making jokes about my own experiences, I didn't really know how to talk about something like this.

As I sat contemplating this, I heard the sound of footsteps not too far in the distance.

Two girls we had gone to school with slowly making their way down the path that cut through the park.

It seemed so long ago now that either of us had sat in a classroom, even though that was exactly where we should have been most days.

I glanced to my cell phone, and as it lit up, I realized it was almost the evening.

That's what I liked most about the summer… the daylight stretched on for hours, giving a sense of adventure to the otherwise boring nights.

I wondered what brought them to this side of town, especially during the summer break. I imagined a nearby party that would be starting soon. Everyone seemed to gravitate towards this side of town to drink.

"Hey," a voiced called casually to us.

As the two girls came closer, I recognized one a little more. Her and I had been quite good friends a couple of years before. I felt a slight pang of sadness seeing her in that moment. Or maybe it was her seeing me. High school dropout, smoking on a park bench in the middle of the afternoon.

Fuck it.

"Haven't seen you in a while," she said, as she walked towards us. Both girls stopped in front us, signalling some kind of interest in a conversation.

"How are you?" I asked, smiling to both of them.

"I'm good," she smiled brightly, tossing a long lock of thick brown hair off her shoulder.

"Are you doing okay though?" she pressed.

She knew I wasn't.

She was one of the only people I had known that had met my family. It seemed like a long time ago now. And I guess it had been. She knew what had happened there, and I always felt a certain sense of caring from her.

"Yeah…. Just trying to figure some things out." I tried to sound confident. This was the closest thing to the truth I could say. Lacking detail and depth, but just enough to alleviate the need for more questioning.

"So, uh… I heard you've been having some fun this summer," she smiled, but not the kind of smile that exuded any kind of warmth.

I watched her face carefully.

My expectations of our prior friendship faded quickly.

"I asked him about it at a party last night," she continued.

I realized suddenly what she was talking about.

Who she was talking about.

"He said it never happened," she said matter-of-factly, a hint of grandiosity in her voice.

Oh.

I sat quietly, fighting the urge to scream.

Ray slid her hand along the park bench, finding mine and gripping it tightly, reminding me she was there. I knew she was confused.

"So what are you doing tonight?" Ray jumped in loudly, saving me from this perceived embarrassment.

The conversation continued for a few more minutes as I stared absently into the line of trees that lay in the distance. Calm and undisturbed. I suddenly couldn't hear the voices surrounding me. Only the one within. The one I could never silence.

Tiles.

Floor.

Shorts.

Blood.

Shut the fuck up.

I closed my eyes tightly for a moment, hoping that would somehow quiet the voice. My voice. The intrusive thoughts constantly threatening my ability to concentrate. On anything.

Tiles.

Cold.

Floor.

Wrists pressing into the stall doors.

Stop.

Please stop.

I would like to tell you that I cried in times like this, but the truth is, I couldn't. Now, when I felt tears rising to the surface, my body stiffened and my mind screamed. I used to be quite an expressive person, but lately I felt like that part of me was slowly slipping away.

But that is the appropriate response, isn't it?

I fall to my knees, unable to bear the weight of the memory.

Cry into my friend's shirt and then promptly call the police.

I'd report everything and would feel such an amazing sense of relief.

The responding officer would become my friend. My mentor.

I would be guided through a court process and would be believed.

Someone would believe me.

And I wouldn't be sick every day with the overwhelming knowledge that no one even understands what happened.

I would stop drinking and shoving pills up my nose to escape it.

To escape everything.

Only now, every hit and every shot served a single, distinct purpose.

If I can't drown myself.

I will drown you.

The memory.

I looked up suddenly, realizing I had removed myself in some form from the conversation. The other girls were several steps away from us now, continuing down the path that led out of the park.

Did I even say goodbye?

"What the fuck was that?"

I jumped, startled, remembering Ray was still sitting beside me.

"So what happened?! You had sex with someone!? I wouldn't lie about something like that, you're hot as fuck," she laughed, but as our eyes met, her smile quickly vanished. She knew something was wrong.

Tell her.

Tell.

Her.

I moved my bag onto my lap, fishing through the contents and pulling out a large bottle of vodka. I had hoped it would last me until tomorrow, but now I knew it probably wouldn't.

I thought about what to say to her. I knew I could tell her. I wasn't worried about that. I just wasn't sure if I could say it out loud without awakening something so dark and destructive inside of myself.

That's the thing when you keep something a secret.

You think it won't eventually destroy you, but it always does.

If I say these words out loud it becomes real outside of my body.

A story for you to take.

And twist.

And tell.

If I say nothing it lives and it grows, delicately contained within the walls of my soul.

Which is worse?

I'm still not sure.

But what I did know was that if I could say it to someone, it could be her.

"It didn't happen that way... I asked him not to," I said quietly.

Silence.

I waited for my body to react.

Should I cry?

Should I be shaking?

Should I throw up?

Should I feel better?

Relieved that I had said it out loud?

Tell me, what is the correct way to grieve?

I felt nothing.

I removed the cap from the vodka and took a long swig, already sensing I was saying too much.

Ray's eyes widened. I knew I didn't' have to say anything else.

She knew now.

Someone knew now.

"He raped y—" her voice was angry, violent even, echoing through the park.

I cut her off before she could finish her sentence.

"Don't say that word," I pleaded quietly.

I wasn't ready for that.

I didn't think I would ever be ready for that.

"I'm sorry." Her voice was shaking, raw with an emotion that I could not emulate. I was jealous of her ability to express things so deeply in that moment.

I watched a tear roll down her face as she tightened her grip on my hand.

I wanted to cry with her.

I desperately wanted to cry with her.

I passed the bottle of vodka over instead.

We both sat in silence for a long time. Breathing in the warm summer night, pondering things quietly and independently, yet together.

After a while I heard her let out a small sigh. She leaned her head onto my shoulder, cuddling into me as we stared off into the distance.

"I'll kill him if I ever see him," she said softly, breaking our long-standing silence.

I wanted to believe that was true.

People say crazy things like that sometimes, and maybe in those moments they mean it.

Maybe.

Ray and I thought the same way. I would have said the same thing if the tables were turned. You do that for your friends, don't you?

It's an unspoken rule.

Align yourself with their pain, their happiness.

Make your presence known in both sorrow and joy.

Just be there.

As we sat there, I thought about what the girl had said.

I wondered what he had been telling people.

I wondered what version of events was quickly making its way through ears only too eager to listen.

I wondered how many of my friends and acquaintances would hear this so-called story.

I wondered how many of them would believe it.

Of course they will.

The voice returned from her momentary rest.

My head began to ache.

Please leave me alone.

You should have fought harder.

I was exhausted thinking of the battle that was about to unfold within my mind. Fighting with myself in complete silence on a park bench.

Like a psychopath.

"Enough," I whispered quietly.

Ray moved her head up from my shoulder, glancing at me.

I must have said that out loud.

"You should come to the alternative school with me in September," she said softly, changing my internal subject for me.

I thought about this for a moment. I really should go back to school, I needed to graduate.

"Yeah, maybe," I said casually, contemplating the weeks ahead.

I wanted to say yes. I wanted to be excited about it... about being around friends again and working towards something as simple as a high school diploma. I wanted to say yes more enthusiastically, but I couldn't. There was something about all of this planning that seemed so out of reach.

Nina had said something about sending me to a treatment centre.

Rehab.

A real rehab.

I didn't like the idea. I told her so.

But as I sat on that park bench thinking about what the next few weeks would hold, I wondered if I would be able to keep myself together.

I wondered if I would continue to just… spiral.

Since moving to this city I felt like something deep inside of me had vanished. Some kind of spirit or energy, maybe. I didn't want to leave our old town. I had finally made friends there… good friends. I was beginning to feel the small tug of roots weaving around me, something I had never experienced before. I wanted so badly to be able to walk into a store or the post office or the grocery store and have the clerks call me by name. Maybe ask how my mother was doing. You know, something that happens when people know you. When my parents sat us all down and announced that we would be moving again, I swear I could feel a little part of myself become lost that day. My few familiarities starting to fade into the background, once again. I didn't want to leave the people I knew, but even more, I didn't want to leave the people who knew me. Again. I didn't have the energy to start over one more time.

Nina had mentioned going to rehab before.

A couple of times.

I didn't really know what an alcoholic or drug addict was… I mean, I had an idea, but the image I had conjured was someone who lived under a bridge downtown, or the beggar on the sidewalk. I wasn't that, but I thought that maybe a warm bed to sleep in and three meals a day wouldn't be so bad. I hadn't slept in a real bed in so long. And maybe I did need a break from the drinking… from everything. I was so tired of the chaotic ways I had been trying to survive.

But more than anything else, I was just tired.

The type of exhaustion that sleep doesn't ever seem to fix.

where do you go when your mind is tired
and your body refuses to rest?
do you lie awake
allowing your soul to scream the memories?
pulling out, one by one, the small shreds of a home you once had
do you wipe your own tears with that same hand?
i hope so
i hope that as these nights pass you by
you begin to remember what happiness feels like
and if that memory evades you
i hope that when you wake
you try your best to create it
happiness

— *glass*

I reached my hand out across the bed, fumbling my fingers frantically around the duvet, attempting to feel where I had put it.

Mirror.

Straw.

Hair tie.

Compact.

Baggie.

BAGGIE.

Got it.

I clutched the flimsy, weathered plastic, my heartbeat finally being advised to retreat from my previous panic.

I rolled slowly onto my back, opening my eyes to meet the ceiling above.

It was perfect. A brilliant white; smooth, but complex.

One of those fancy, complicated swirling designs that you only see in homes that are either very old or owned by the very rich.

The house was set neatly in a picturesque area of the city I didn't venture to often.

In fact, I never came here unless it was to see Vee.

I often wondered what his parents thought of him.

Of us.

Did they know he was a drug dealer?

Did they care?

Did they even suspect it?

He was only nineteen after all.

His mother seemed to be the type who would look away at any mention of trouble.

Pretending that everything and everyone was okay.

More than okay.

Perfect.

And his father appeared to be the kind of man who would sooner buy his son's affection rather than take interest in his day-to-day experiences.

The rich boy wasn't so rich.

I felt bad for him sometimes.

Light was beginning to spill into the room from the windows that enclosed this humble but bustling space.

Morning.

It's already morning.

I took a deep breath in, inviting the overwhelming sense of dread that often accompanied a comedown of this sort.

Just as I began to push myself to a sitting position, the door to the bedroom opened swiftly.

Vee walked in, ignoring my presence, as he made his way over to the couch in the small corner of the room, opening a laptop and pressing play on his usual morning-after playlist.

Radiohead.

I didn't understand how on earth someone could listen to this for hours on end while fighting the devastating emotional downward spiral that came after a night of doing ecstasy.

"I've got some things to do today," he said flatly, not looking up from his computer.

He wanted me to go.

That was obvious.

I moved myself towards the edge of the bed, gathering my belongings which were scattered within the sheets.

I wouldn't argue with him.

I thought about the things I needed to do today.

Hop a bus and somehow find my way back to the other end of the city, steal some food for dinner later and make sure I had enough of whatever I needed to make it through the evening.

And what I needed was illegal and frowned upon.

It was going to be a busy day.

I opened my bag and began throwing my belongings inside.

Loudly.

As I reached for my wallet, I fumbled with it, watching it fall from my grasp and land beside a small wastebasket.

I reached down to grab it, glancing at the contents in the open garbage can.

A condom.

Not just a condom, a used condom.

I felt a sudden burst of jealousy.

Not because he was clearly having sex with someone — someone who wasn't me — but because I suddenly didn't like the thought of another girl laying next to him. In the spot where I was now.

In that moment I wondered if that's why he always seemed so irritated the mornings after we spent time together.

I didn't allow him to touch me like that.

And I liked him.

There was no doubt that I liked him.

I just always envisioned my first time doing something like that being with someone who cared about me.

It's never been about "saving myself" for someone.

I'm not a cupcake.

I just wanted to know that whoever I shared that with at least wanted the best for me.

And I had not yet felt that with anyone.

I knew I didn't have a right to be upset with him.

I came here for comfort; we both knew that.

To lay beside each other in a warm bed, safely tucked away from the noise.

To pretend that just for a short time, things were okay.

He didn't tell me much about his life, and he didn't ask much about mine.

It was nice.

And I needed that right now.

I needed someone to lay beside me, demanding nothing, and help me to forget.

I could suddenly feel him looking over at me.

Watching me stare a little too long into the contents of that bin.

"Do you want me to walk you to the bus?"

He knew what I had seen.

And judging by this kind offer, I think it was something he hadn't wanted me to see.

But I guess that's what happens when you're too high to let the maid in to clean your room.

"No."

My reply was cool, forcing him to try a little harder to gain my attention.

"I see other people sometimes," he laughed, trying his best to compose himself as he stood up from the couch, moving towards me slowly, unsure if he should.

"It's not like we're together...," he continued.

He's right.

Oh great, now you're getting involved too?

"And you're a virgin anyways." I could tell as soon as the words fell off of his tongue, he regretted it.

But as that word moved through the room, there was a heaviness about it that pressed itself down on my chest.

An aching sadness that I had been trying so hard not to think about.

You're not a virgin anymore.

The images returned rapidly, flashing through my mind.

Tiles.

Floor.

Cold.

Stop, I silently demanded, hoping my inner voice would be drowned out. Somehow.

"I'm not," I began quietly. I didn't know why I was telling him that.

Don't.

Her tone was firm.

Say nothing more.

I looked over to him. Watching him stare, waiting for me to elaborate.

I tried to relax my shoulders as I cleared my throat. My eyes glanced around the room avoiding but finally falling back to his.

Maybe I could tell him.

We were friends, weren't we?

Or maybe you just want him to do something about it?

To save you?

Pathetic.

He won't.

And you'll look like an attention-seeking whore.

Stop.

If I ever want to be anything more to him, I should at least tell him something, I thought to myself.

"It happened a couple weeks ago… I was hanging out with someone at—" I began, trying to find the words.

The right words.

But not the truth.

"So you're not a virgin anymore?" He cut me off, the irritation in his voice returning.

He turned his back to me, retracing his steps towards the couch, but not sitting down.

He picked up a pair of glasses that lay on the coffee table and put them on, adjusting them to his face before letting out a quiet sigh.

"I guess that's that then," he said, ending the conversation.

He looked over to me, his eyes displaying a mix of contempt and disappointment.

Was this what I had been to him all this time?

A customer turned companion who had quickly turned into a wasted opportunity?

Because virgins are pure, right?

Clean?

And I was not that anymore.

You idiot.

He's a drug dealer.

A fuckin drug dealer.

He's not your friend.

I didn't want to listen to her right now.

Not today.

This casual voice inside of me that offered reality in its harshest forms at times.

"Well, as I said, I have things to do today," he said, motioning towards the door.

I felt my heartbeat quicken as I fumbled with something to say.

But there was nothing.

Nothing for me here.

And certainly nothing left to say.

I made my way out of his room, down the staircase and around the corner to make my way to the side door of the house.

The one we usually came in and out of.

As I approached the door, I heard a small, feeble voice behind me.

"Goodbye."

I turned quickly to see Vee's mother looking over to me from a small leather chair in the living room that was angled in such a way that she could see the door clearly, although I wasn't sure if anyone else was in the room with her.

I didn't even realize she was home.

Although it wasn't uncommon for her to be sitting somewhere in the house. Saying and doing nothing.

Drinking her wine and staring absently into her perfectly decorated walls.

Come to think of it, this was the first time she had acknowledged me.

I nodded to her, examining her face.

She looked sad.

Maybe she was hoping I would say something to her.

Strike up a conversation, sit with her in her silence.

"I think you left your toothbrush in the bathroom, dear," she pointed a delicately-manicured hand towards the powder room that sat adjacent to the exit.

I had never used that bathroom before.

She must have realized this as she surveyed my expression.

"Or perhaps it was the other girl," she said quietly as she turned from me, lifting a fancy porcelain cup to her lips.

Bitch.

Perhaps I had read her wrong.

I adjusted my bag on my shoulder, confused by what had just happened.

I moved towards the door and placed my hand on the rounded chrome handle, one that seemed too simple and out of place for an estate like this.

I related to it for a moment.

The door handle.

As I stepped out into the morning, the sunshine brushed across my face, trying the way it does to bring me some kind of warmth.

With every step I took the emotions seemed to reach up, one by one, grabbing me by the throat and twisting.

Twisting.

And I could feel it starting to happen again.

My mind panned back vividly to the cold tiles.

The blood.

The shorts.

The words.

His words.

"No one is ever gonna know."

But you know.

It was then that I realized I had a bottle of vodka stuffed in the bottom of my bag. It was also then that I realized there was no need to rush my tired feet back to the other side of the city.

No one was looking for me.

when it's 3 a.m. in your tiny apartment
and you are drunk with the love of your life
i hope you think of me
i hope that as you dance in the middle of your living room
swaying from side to side
wrapping your arms around her
the wind ejects itself from your lungs
as you remember what you've done
i hope you attempt to create a life so beautiful
that when you burn it to the ground
with your self-delusion and destruction
you will feel true pain
and i hope you live to be one hundred and ten
spending all of your lonely days and nights
tossing and turning in the silent chaos
knowing that you will never escape the memory
and knowing that I have forgotten that i exist

— remember me

The lights inside the bus were harsher than I remembered.

Or maybe I was just sober.

Too sober.

The bus rumbled through the familiar neighbourhood, bouncing and swaying gently on the uneven pavement below.

I was on my way to see Ray and her boyfriend.

By this time in the evening I was sure more friends would be gathering with them soon. It was a half-hour bus ride on a good day, and in hindsight I probably could have just walked there faster.

The bus route streamed through three different residential neighbourhoods, which was time consuming, but I liked it because it gave me time to write and listen to music.

I loved the buses for that.

I would slide myself down in the seat, lifting my knees up and pressing them on the back of the awkward metal seat in front of me.

This would hurt my knees if I did it for too long, but I didn't mind.

More recently I had been finding comfort in holding things to my chest.

My knees, my bag, a pillow.

I'm not sure why, but it made me feel somehow more comfortable.

Safer, maybe.

On this particular evening I was more tired than usual.

I hadn't had anything to eat or drink today, and the longer it took me to get to Ray made me doubt whether she would have anything left for me. I knew she always tried to save some vodka, but it was late and I was... not myself.

I had a feeling it would take much more than what she had left
to get me where I wanted to be.

Where I needed to be.

Numb.

It seemed to be taking more and more these days to achieve that.

I glanced out the window and squinted, trying to recognize
where I was.

Once I saw the sign for the little church on the corner, I knew I
was close.

There.

I pulled the bell, signalling to the driver that I was getting off at
the next stop.

I walked towards the front of the bus to exit. Most people got
off at the back, but there was no one else on this bus tonight,
and besides, Mark was driving.

Mark drove three of the bus routes on this side of town.

I had met him for the first time when I was fourteen and brand
new to the city. Filled with the usual teenage anxieties.

Also, I had never taken a city bus before.

Mark was an older man, maybe early sixties, although I couldn't
tell. He kept himself in remarkable shape. If I was ever going
to have a crush on an older man, it would have been him. He
had a deep, booming voice which he used to announce each
upcoming stop. Street names and all. Most of the other drivers
didn't do that.

Over the years I found myself getting onto Mark's buses at
various hours throughout both night and day.

The night I left home I had been walking down a road close
to my parents' house. My face was still hot and momentarily
weathered from all the screaming. I had a backpack that had

been filled hastily with clothing and nothing else. No bus fare. Mark saw me as he drove his regular route up that same street. He stopped the bus beside me, no actual bus stop in sight. The long and narrow bus door opened and a warm, concerned voice spilled out.

"You need a ride?"

When he wasn't announcing bus stops, his voice was actually quite soothing.

"I don't have any tickets," I had called back.

Mark smiled and made a summoning motion with his hand.

He had no idea what had happened that night and he didn't ask, but he made sure I got to the other side of town safely.

After that, Mark seemed to take a liking to me and I to him, as we developed an odd sort of friendship.

I spent many nights walking down a dimly-lit road at some ungodly hour only to be met by Mark, who opened his bus door and ushered me inside.

Into safety.

I was grateful for him, and on his routes, I always went to the front of the bus to exit so I could say thank you. And so he could tell me to stay out of trouble.

"I'll try," I would reply, both of us smiling to each other.

I stepped out into the night, zipping up my sweater to escape the slightly cooler breeze. From here I would need to walk another twenty minutes to get to Ray. I began my descent down the street which passed by my old school.

It was hard to think that I had been removed from there for so long now.

Not that I wanted to go back, but I wondered what the next year would have looked like if I had stayed.

Preparing for prom, writing final exams, signing yearbooks.

You wouldn't have done that shit anyways.

She was right, I probably wouldn't have.

And I felt a slight shudder of sadness at that thought.

Maybe if you could stop fuckin up, you could have done all those things.

Maybe.

The lights surrounding the school never seemed to shine too brightly.

The awkwardly-shaped building appeared like some kind of oversized and haunted bungalow.

I continued down the sidewalk towards a beacon of flickering streetlights ahead.

As I neared the flow of light streaming onto the pavement, I heard voices.

They all seemed to be speaking at once.

Laughing and yelling obnoxiously over one another.

Boys.

There was a convenience store on the corner I was approaching, and as I grew closer, so did the voices.

I stepped below a steady stream of light cascading down from a streetlight above me, announcing my presence silently, as the group of boys peered up from their banter.

I looked at them, surveying the faces.

Recognizing.

His friends.

Many of them.

Here.

I glanced behind me quickly to see if anyone else was walking this way.

Anyone I knew.

Someone.

Anyone.

My heart felt like it was about to pound straight out of my chest.

One of them stood up from the sidewalk and moved towards me, and as he gained ground, I stopped.

I had seen this boy before. Many times.

We travelled in some of the same circles, only really talking to each other in passing. He had always been friendly to me.

Almost a friend.

"Haven't seen you in a while," he said. It was slightly genuine.

"Yeah, I've been busy," I replied quickly.

Busy doing what?

All you've been doing is drinking.

Fuck off.

"Where are you going?" he asked casually, his voice a little lighter.

Maybe sensing my nervousness.

"Just meeting some people over there," I motioned towards the ballpark in the distance, hoping he wouldn't ask anything more specific.

"Cool... be careful."

I locked eyes with him then.

There was something about the way he said it that didn't sit right with me.

He took a step backwards, slowly, not breaking eye contact, as if allowing me to leave.

It was obvious in that moment that the one I was trying to avoid wasn't there.

It was also obvious that people were talking. In secret and in groups.

The rest of the boys who remained sitting and prancing around the convenience store had continued on with their conversations, uninterested in ours.

I repositioned my bag on my shoulder and turned, aiming myself towards my next destination, but before I could take a step, he continued, only louder this time.

"Don't get too wild, eh?" There was laughter in his voice.

He knew.

Why the fuck would he say that to me?

He told him.

He knew.

I turned around quickly.

What's your move?

What are you gonna say to that?

I silently wished that for once this unrelenting bitch would give me some solid advice rather than being a seemingly useless bit of commentary.

I didn't know what to say.

But I knew I didn't want to sound or appear the least bit bothered.

"Yeah, I guess I wouldn't want to be in another fucked up situation again," I laughed.

A fake, high pitched, sarcastic, clumsy laugh.

Excuse me?

Why are you trying to make a joke about this?

It's not funny.

WHAT THE FUCK IS WRONG WITH YOU?

I've got this.

I fuckin hope so.

The words I had chosen irritated him.

It left too much room to imply that I didn't like what had happened that night.

"You need to be careful what you say." His voice was aggressive, and he took a step towards me as if recalculating how close he should be.

"I don't know what you're talking about," I spat.

"You and I both know that's not what happened. You followed him in there, you were fuckin making out with him all night." Before I could say anything, he turned away from me and walked back towards the group, some of whom were listening now.

I stood for a moment, staring at the back of his head as he walked, wondering what to say.

What could I say?

Say nothing.

Get out of here.

I turned around and began walking, quickly, barely looking at my surroundings but focusing on my feet and my breath.

I must have been holding it.

I blew out the stagnant air from my lungs and inhaled quickly, trying to restore my composure.

I was walking in the wrong direction, but I didn't care, I just needed to get away.

He's going to tell everyone you wanted it to happen.

I know.

People are going to think you're a whore.

"I was a virgin," I choked. Tears threatened to spring up behind my eyes.

Even worse.

I knew Ray would be wondering what happened to me. I thought about calling her, but I didn't have enough minutes left on my phone. And besides, what do I say?

It wasn't just her at the spot tonight.

There would be more people, and most of them were either friends with him or knew him well enough.

And how do I compete with that?

I had only been living here for three years.

Most of the people I was friends with — we were friends with — had lived here their whole lives. They had known him since elementary school.

So who do you think they would believe?

The drunk runaway or the charming boy?

There's nothing charming about him, I snapped back to myself.

Not to you.

But then again, there's nothing charming about you either, is there?

Just leave me alone, I pleaded quietly.

Fine.

There's cough medicine in the bag.

Relief.

The tension throughout my body began to dissipate, slowly, but then faster with that realization.

If you drink enough of it, you'll probably just blackout.

Good, I thought.

I had discovered cough medicine recently, and that if you do everything but follow the dosing instructions, it could be useful in emergencies.

The types of emergencies that never involved a cough or cold.

The kind of emergencies when you are alone with your thoughts and your stomach begins to sink and shake and you feel like you might be sick.

When you miss your parents and your brother and sister so much but know you can't go back home.

When you realize there isn't enough money to buy food or alcohol or bus tickets so you steal, and the shame of who you are becoming seeps in.

When the nightmares begin and as you wake, remembering every detail, you promise yourself you will find a way to quiet that space in your mind just enough to rest.

When you miss something you've never experienced.

When you want to go home.

Those kinds of emergencies.

There was a bus shelter around the corner; I could go there.

You need to get farther away.

From them.

She was right.

As I continued walking away aimlessly, I realized there really was nowhere in this suburban landscape I could go without risking running into someone from that crowd.

One of his friends.

One of our friends.

Him.

I wondered how long it would take for the rumours to spread. After what happened tonight, I imagined his friend would quickly warn him about our encounter.

Maybe this would make him sharpen his story even more.

Deny it ever happened or deny how it happened.

Whatever happened now, it would at least be known that there were two sides to the story.

And yours will be forgotten.

I tripped on an uneven piece of sidewalk, stumbling slightly before regaining my balance.

I could hear the small clink of the bottle of cough medicine against the metal clasp on my wallet inside my bag.

Reminding me silently that while I may be losing hope, I could at least spend the remainder of this evening blissfully unaware.

As I walked, I realized the road was soon coming to an end.

A set of traffic lights announced the only options of going either right or left.

If I turned right, I would be met with the road that would lead me back towards where I was staying… close to where my parents still lived… and close to where it happened.

If I turned left, I would be presented with a long, straight, main drag, which would pass by a mall before descending along a line of townhouses. Almost as far as the eye could see.

If I turned left, I could go to the little strip mall which also had a bus stop.

Many different routes passed through this makeshift station.

Many different routes, going many different places.

Where are you going to go?

Anywhere but here.

I turned left.

how careless you become when you aren't cared for
how unloving you can be when you aren't loved
but I wonder
when the snake bites you
how you've become the venom and not the dead

— snakes

I pulled the curtain closed tightly.

I wasn't sure exactly what I thought I would achieve by doing that.

It was so bright outside today, and the curtain was white, uselessly transparent.

My eyes were aching from the intrusive rays trying their best to creep into the little bathroom.

What time was it?

I heard the door handle start the jiggle and a small voice from the other side whisper, "Sorry," as little footsteps scurried away.

It was one of her children.

The lady who was letting me live here.

I wasn't the only one in the house, in fact; it was usually filled with several of us, usually on different floors.

I wondered how she managed it most days.

A single mother looking after four kids, one of which wasn't even hers.

She was a kind, quiet lady who had shown me nothing but love and understanding.

And naturally, I had no idea what to do with that.

So I stayed quiet, did dishes, cleaned bathrooms and promised myself I wouldn't drink in her house. A promise I didn't always keep.

You're out of everything.

It was obviously early enough that my inner voice had awoken.

Reminding me that my bag was empty, I had no money, and there was really nowhere to go today.

I thought about who I could call to get something.

Anything.

What would be the cheapest?

Weed, I guess.

I didn't really like weed unless I was alone.

I always felt it made me paranoid and awkward, more insecure than usual.

But it would also put me to sleep faster than anything else, and I quite enjoyed being unconscious these days.

I looked over to the other side of the bathroom where my clean clothes lay on the floor.

I should get dressed and get moving, I thought to myself.

And the other kids obviously needed to get in here too.

I moved over to the clothing quickly and started getting dressed.

I pulled my jeans up, and as I looked over to where my hairbrush was, I caught a glimpse of myself in the mirror.

It took me by surprise.

I hadn't looked at myself in long time.

Really looked at myself.

My hair was getting longer.

I was getting thinner.

I ran my hand along my rib cage, feeling the curve of each bone before guiding myself down to my stomach, along my hips.

My hips.

Floor.

Tiles.

Blood.

A group of images from that night flashed through my mind.

Again.

I thought back to the other night when I had run into his friend.

And the days before that seeing the girls in the park.

I wondered if anyone was thinking about what had happened.

Questioning his story.

Probably not.

They're going to think you're a liar, and he will get away with it.

That's not fair, though.

Oh Hunnie… no one cares if it's fair, she laughed.

In that moment I wanted to see his face.

I wanted to see him look at me and watch his posture shift, his eyes look away in shame and embarrassment.

I wanted him to fuckin look at me and realize what happened.

What he did.

Oh he knows… and he doesn't care.

Shut up.

I grabbed my cell phone, which lay open on the edge of the sink in front of me, quickly pulling up my contacts.

He was in there.

He had weed.

I could get him to sell me something, meet me somewhere and then I could talk to him.

Confront him.

And what the fuck are you going to say?

I don't know.

It doesn't matter.

I'll figure it out, but I need to see his face.

I need to know that he knows.

If no one else will believe it, I at least need to fuckin know that he knows.

This is a bad idea.

I didn't want to argue with her today, with myself.

My heart began to race, hands shaking as I hovered a finger over his name.

Call.

The phone started ringing.

I held my breath as I put the phone up to my ear.

Just as the third ring was beginning, the line went cold.

Straight to voicemail.

He's ignoring you.

I pulled the phone down and hit redial.

The line began to ring again, this time only once before ending.

Voicemail again.

He's fuckin ignoring you.

I felt the blood rushing to my face as an odd sensation came over my body.

One I would usually abruptly try to control. Anger.

Redial.

Ring.

Voicemail.

Redial.

Ring.

Voicemail.

Redial.

Ring. Voicemail.

The tears began to form as I felt my body ache and contort with the very knowledge that he was ignoring me.

Still.

Discarding me the way he had that night.

Stop this.

Redial.

Ring.

"Hello?"

I held my breath again, this time suddenly.

I wasn't prepared for him to answer.

"I need…. I need to buy something."

My voice was quiet. Timid.

Too quiet.

Make yourself sound more confident.

"I can't meet you right now," he said coldly, an air or irritation in his voice.

"What about in a couple hours?" I asked, trying to assert myself before he had the chance to decline again.

"I need something today. I can meet you somewhere close, I have cash."

Silence.

I pulled the phone from my face quickly to look at the screen, thinking he had hung up.

He hadn't.

Not yet.

"Yeah," he sighed.

I could feel his disapproval.

"Meet me where we were at the other night. Two hours."

The line went dead.

Before I could stop myself, I watched suddenly as my arm threw the phone across the bathroom. It cracked as it hit the opposing wall and fell swiftly into a pile of laundry on the floor.

He wants to meet there?

You shouldn't go back there.

This isn't right.

Fuck it.

I pulled myself up, realizing I must have crouched down at some point during the phone calls.

As I stood, I felt as if the wind had been knocked out of me.

I pressed my hands on either side of the bathroom sink, steadying myself as I tried to direct my breathing, which was slowly retreating to a calm and steady rhythm. I felt control. I will make him look at me. I will make him see me.

i will run through these streets every night
begging the lights to guide me home
and as you stumble from that walkway
and we lock eyes in the middle of this storm
you will wonder where i've been
you will try to ask the question
but beneath your curiosity
will be all your reservations held for me
and we will pass like ships in the night
too scared to reach
too young to try

— another life

I opened the café door and stepped inside, my body welcoming the cool air as it soaked into my skin.

It was warmer than usual today, even for the summer.

And I had been walking for what felt like a long time.

I glanced around the small café, nervously scanning the customers one by one.

He wasn't here.

He's not coming.

The cashier looked over to me, waiting for me to approach her to order something.

I pulled my phone out of my pocket, pretending to read something as I stepped away from the line of customers that I was obviously in the way of.

This wasn't the kind of place where you had to buy something in order to stay, but I also didn't want to stay here any longer than planned.

I thought about what I would say to him.

He would be here any minute.

I needed to think of something.

I searched the room around me again, watching the various groups and sets of people sitting happily, conversing with one another.

As I watched their faces, trying to imagine what they were talking about, what their plans were for the day, I was distracted by the door that sat stiffly in the far corner of the room.

Tiles.

Cold.

Floor.

Blood.

Where it happened.

I knew my body and my mind would react to this.

This space.

I had tried to prepare myself for it in the hours leading up to coming here.

Now that I was here, I felt desperately out of place.

Why are you like this?

Dramatic, stupid girl.

Always jumping before you fuckin look.

Please stop, I pleaded to myself, holding my hands together tightly, trying to simultaneously stop the shaking while pulling whatever air I could find into my lungs.

Slowly.

Steadily.

I looked again to the people sitting, talking, laughing.

How odd it felt in that moment that this space was simultaneously holding so much pain for me and so much normalcy for them.

Their simple afternoon coffee with friends.

And the runaway in the corner.

This is what's wrong with you.

Shut up.

Impulsive, silly whore.

This is exactly what the fuck is wrong with you.

You probably wanted it to happen.

"Please stop," I choked, pushing out another uselessly unmeditative breath.

"Hey."

I felt an arm reach over my shoulder, pulling me in to a sideways hug.

My shoulders shot up as I realized who was touching me.

I stepped back from the embrace immediately, all of the air rushing from my lungs as I stumbled back slightly.

"I — here," I fumbled, pushing a clutched twenty-dollar bill to him.

Get the fuck out of here.

"You uh, doing anything today?" he was trying his best to speak casually, his hands moving quickly as he passed a small plastic bag over to me, which I grabbed quickly, pushing into my bag.

He wouldn't look at me.

He wouldn't fuckin look at me.

I suddenly didn't realize why I was here.

Why I had thought this would accomplish anything.

You fuckin idiot.

"Um, no, not really, just go see Ray I think."

I stared at him. Watching his eyes dart along the floor between us, refusing to look up.

To look at me.

"Alright, well, uh. Listen, if you need anything else let me know."

I won't.

Before I could begin to take a full breath, he was gone.

I watched, in slow motion, as the door to the café closed behind him.

Well, look at you.

Please, just stop.

Did you get what you wanted?

Why did you do that?

I don't know.

But that's what I wanted to ask him.

That's the only thing I had wanted to say.

i threw myself from my tower that day
gracefully racing towards the ground
wondering the whole way down
would you catch me if you're near?
do you even know i'm here?
and they warned me in their whispers and their laughs
there is no one coming
no one coming
and as i fell towards the ground
my eyes adjusting to the black
the angels swung their needles down
and the wings were sewn onto my back

— every time the bell rings

Nina had been in my life for three years.

I knew it was three years because I met her when I was fourteen.

I also knew it was three years because I hadn't known many people for that long.

So I kept track.

When I was younger, I used to have a little notepad where I would write the names of people I would meet, mostly friends at school.

I would make a little tally beside their names, and each mark would represent one year.

No one ever made it past three marks.

Nina was the only person in my life who I could say anything and everything to. In an honest way.

Not the way I did with my friends where I would make jokes about things that hurt me or exaggerate funny stories.

With Nina, I could tell her when I was scared or when I felt lost or when I wanted to die, and she would sit, quietly, never breaking her gaze from me.

And she didn't take notes during our sessions.

I liked that.

When you become a fuck up at school, sometimes they will try to give you a guidance counsellor, but when you start doing drugs at school, they will give you an addictions counsellor.

Mine was Nina.

On that particular afternoon, Nina was coming to see me at the house.

Something most counsellors didn't do, however, I hadn't been to school in months.

It would have been quite easy for her to close my file.

I'm sure she could have written a final note about how I "no longer met the criteria" as I was no longer a student.

But she didn't.

In recent weeks, we would meet in random little coffee shops or restaurants.

I'm sure people probably thought we were sisters or old friends.

She didn't seem like the typical counsellor.

I had always pictured a counsellor or therapist to be some middle-aged man or woman, authoritative and tired.

Tired of dealing with people's shit.

I had guessed that is what a job like that would eventually do.

Especially when looking after teenagers.

But Nina's eyes were alive and bright with care, and she had an astonishing ability to tell you the harsher truths of your thoughts or behaviour while allowing you to sink into a deep feeling of comfort.

Her very presence was comforting.

Sometimes I would ask her about her life outside of being my counsellor; she was someone I would have wanted to spend time with.

We had built a strange kind of friendship.

One that I could see her trying to manage on a professional level, being careful not to divulge too much about herself, but sometimes our conversations would trail off and I would find her telling me little things about her life.

It made me feel like I was sitting with someone I really knew and not just another number on her caseload.

I loved hearing her talk about her life.

It was a nice break from talking about mine.

I would sip the fancy coffees she would buy me, getting lost in all the little details of her life.

Hearing her complain about her old shitty car that always made a bit too much noise when it started.

You had to give the passenger door an extra kick to get it open. I liked it.

It was grimy and real and held all the realities of trying to get by in life.

Her boyfriend had proposed recently, and it made me happy to think she would be starting on this new chapter of her life, one filled with love and hope and promise.

Sometimes when she would tell me these little things, my mind would wander off to a different place.

I would think about what it would be like to finish school, to get my first car, my first real job.

I thought about what it would feel like to be in love.

I wanted that so badly.

To have someone to climb into a warm bed with, whispering these same little stories to.

Telling jokes and kissing each other and feeling like there was nothing in the whole entire world that could possibly go all that wrong as long as I had this person beside me.

I wanted someone to be happy to see me.

I think sometimes when you want something that badly, you don't often look correctly at the people you meet.

Any of the boys I had liked, or the ones who had shown interest in me, I seemed to cling to, like a child.

This desperate hope that they would become the person I was imagining, and that I could shift myself into what I thought they wanted.

The great chameleon.

I wanted somebody to see me, and stay.

The one who would take me away from everything I was drowning in.

And I think we all want that, don't we?

But sometimes I could no longer tell if I wanted someone to fix the things I couldn't or simply stay with me as I tried to fix them myself.

Either way, it is a different kind of heartache when someone reaches out to you and you can no longer see their soul, just a shadow of all the things you hope they will be.

A blurry, eerie image of careful expectations.

And I seemed to always say too much.

Giving away too much information, spilling all the things I hated or loved or felt scared about.

Trying to crash into someone in hopes that they would crash into me back.

Maybe I was just looking for myself.

When you are young, you don't know yet that you will eventually become the hero in your own story.

"I'm worried about you," Nina said softly, placing her purse down at her feet as she sat on the edge of the small couch in the living room, waiting for me to join her.

The sun was trying its best to peek through the small cracks in the mess of curtains that hung unevenly, covering the little bay window that sat behind her.

I thought about opening them, more for her comfort than mine, but it was too bright out.

Even for 10 a.m. on a Tuesday.

"I'm okay," I said, without making eye contact as I sunk into the seat cushion beside her.

You've always been a terrible liar.

She waited for me to continue.

She always did that.

It's like she knew I wouldn't be able to handle the silence and would eventually begin talking in circles, leading to something interesting.

Something real.

The truth.

I guess that is a fairly useful tactic, but today I couldn't find the energy to say anything.

The silence felt... good... for once.

No one was home in the house, and I hadn't heard it this quiet in weeks.

I felt her shift as she reached down into her purse and pull out a pamphlet of some kind.

But not the kind you see in dental offices, printed on some heavier kind of paper, with brilliantly clear images.

This one had obviously been printed from a computer and folded hastily.

She held it out to me, and as I scanned the front page, I realized what it was. Information on a treatment centre.

The one she had been telling me about a few weeks ago.

I stared blankly at the image in front of me as my hands moved to begin unfolding the rest of it.

"You could go next week," she said softly.

Waiting for me to give some kind of sign of approval, or even acknowledgment.

"They have a bed ready for you. You would just need to detox first… there are places that can help with that."

I stared at the pamphlet, glancing over the different boxes one by one, each seeming to offer some kind of relief to the current life of the reader.

I wondered what it would be like going there.

Leaving here.

I had been running full speed away from everything that had been uncomfortable over the last few years.

I had tried going back home a few times.

Back to my parents.

Each time things seemed to get worse.

And how do you explain that to someone?

That the one place you are supposed to feel loved, and the place you are supposed to be able to love had slowly turned to sand.

Drifting through the cracks in my fingers.

I didn't recognize my family anymore.

My parents drowned their sorrows in both alcohol and isolation.

The tides of life and their own demons catching up with them.

Losing themselves a little bit more each day.

Or that's how it looked.

I wondered how it must have felt.

For them.

I remember looking at my brother across the dinner table one night so many months ago.

He had been staring at a napkin on the table, but not in the kind of way that made you think he was thinking about the napkin.

No, he was far away that evening.

The voices of our parents were growing louder around us, but I could not stop staring at my brother as he kept his eyes frozen on that fuckin napkin.

And then suddenly, quietly, I saw him begin to open his mouth ever so slowly, as he said to us but also to no one, "What do you think is the fastest way to kill yourself?"

There was a cold and immediate silence that hung over us then as I felt my fork drop down beside my plate, my mouth dropped open and I looked at either side of me to my parents.

Say something.

Their eyes glanced from one another and then across the table, scanning the carefully laid items.

Doing anything to avoid a conversation.

The conversation.

Your son wants to die…. Say something.

But that silence lingered for longer than it should have before the voices around us slowly grew again, carrying on with their conversation.

I wanted to say something.

I desperately wanted to find the words to comfort him.

I wanted to scream at my parents for not seeing us, not hearing us.

But like them, I said nothing.

I couldn't find the words.

I didn't know where to put his pain.

Where do you put the rest of the pain when you've run out of room?

I was never as brave as I thought I was.

My brother looked up to me, finally, and as our eyes connected, I realized those once brilliant blues were dark and cloudy.

The conversation around us continued as the words fluttered around us, uselessly oblivious.

He nodded to me, lifelessly, as he picked up the little white napkin in front of him, crumpling it into a ball and tossing it on his plate.

He placed both hands on the table's edge and gently pushed his chair back, excusing himself from the meal.

My heart began to race realizing our parents weren't done eating yet.

He wasn't supposed to leave the table until they were done, that's the rule.

We all knew that.

But on that night, they didn't seem to notice.

It's funny how you can live with the same people for years... sit across tables and eat meals together and share space together and still have no idea who they are. It scared me.

As he walked up the stairs, I watched my mother break away momentarily from whatever conversation she was having with my father.

Her eyes followed my brother's footsteps up the stairs, trailing off into the darkened hallway.

We listened as the door to his room closed.

Go talk to him.

As if she was listening to my thoughts, my mother turned her gaze towards me, nodding silently, fresh tears softly lining the bottom of her eyes.

Why can't any of you just fuckin talk to each other?

I don't know.

I don't know.

"What do you think?" Nina asked quietly, bringing me back to our conversation.

I let out a long, slow breath before passing the pamphlet back to her.

Let's get out of here.

The funny thing about that inner voice is that she can simultaneously want me to live while also demanding that I kill some part of myself.

The part that hurts.

Whatever her motive was today, we agreed on something for once.

I needed to get out of here.

I looked to Nina, surveying her face and noticing something I didn't quite realize I had been looking for.

She saw me in this moment.

She had seen me in many moments before this.

Maybe — just maybe — she knew what she was doing.

Maybe she does know what's best for me right now.

I nodded to her, watching her shoulders relax with my quiet acceptance.

resting on the surface
pushing your weight into mine
but never merging together
i will carry you next to me
no matter how delicate you seem
and they will scream to us to part
you're killing me
and saving my life
all at once

— oil and water

"You look much better these days, Darlin."

I looked up from my journal to see Silva opening the rickety screen door that led out to the deck.

I jumped up to grab it for her as she placed one foot down on the old wooden floorboards, steadying herself with her cane.

"No, no, no," she huffed, trying to swipe my hand away as she took a step forward. "I'm just fine, Hunnie, you sit down."

Her voice was the kind of harsh that only comes with large amounts of alcohol, cigarettes and time, but for some reason, I found it comforting all the same.

I moved back to where I had been sitting and pulled another old plastic chair closer to me so Silva could sit.

Silva was in her sixties. Older than most of us here, but you almost couldn't tell. Whenever I saw her, she always had a full face of make-up on, including bright red lipstick, accompanied by a large mane of distressed looking bleach blonde locks tied up high in a chaotic ponytail.

I liked her.

She was messy and exciting and expressive.

She was loud and opinionated and alive.

I wanted to be more like Silva.

I think I was once.

Before life happened and I somehow decided that being small and quiet and dishonest was better.

Safer.

She lowered herself slowly into the chair beside me, letting out a long, loud sigh as she rested her cane down between us.

I made the mistake of asking her if her leg was okay one day, and she started yelling about how the cops in her city beat women like her.

Prostitutes.

Her leg had never been the same after the last one.

She and I spent hours sitting on the old back porch, sharing cigarettes and talking about life.

She had so many stories from over the years and was a phenomenal storyteller. Some evenings there would be seven or eight of us out here, all sitting quietly in a big circle as Silva shared another insane tale about her life years ago.

Once upon a time she had been a fashion designer.

A very successful one.

"If I woke up and wanted a new pair of shoes, I would do a big breakfast line of coke and fly to Milan!" she exclaimed one night, filling the darkness around us with laughter and images of her adventures.

Her stories were outrageous, and I never quite knew if all of them were true, but judging by the place we all ended up, I guess it didn't matter now.

"What are you writing about today, Sweetheart?" she asked warmly, leaning overly slightly to glance at my journal.

Nothing, because you can't think straight.

I noticed then that the page was blank.

I had been sitting out here for an hour.

It was Sunday, and we had a lot of free time on weekends.

Well, as free as it can be in rehab.

"Nothing yet," I said, a hint of frustration crept into my voice as I closed the journal and placed it on the little plastic coffee table in front of us.

Why couldn't I write?

It was always something that brought me comfort, and up until today I had been writing every day since coming here.

My mind felt sharper than it had in ages.

At the end of the day when our therapy was over, I would wait until after dinner and then come sit on the deck and write for hours, but today, nothing seemed to be coming out.

"I can't," I said quietly, tossing the pen onto the table beside the notebook.

Silva leaned back in her chair and looked at me curiously.

"Well, Baby girl, maybe you're not supposed to write anything today…. Maybe you'd be better off sitting here with me, looking at the river."

I looked out through the field that led from the back porch down to a large flowing river tucked away neatly behind a large line of trees about three hundred feet away from where we sat.

"We can't see it from here," I laughed, pointing to the treeline.

"But you know it's there, don't you?" Silva smiled.

She was right.

I could tell we were close to water when we arrived, even before I knew where the water was.

You could smell it in the air, feel it on your skin, even from all the way back here.

"Kind of like this big old universe, isn't it, Hunnie?"

"What do you mean?" I asked, curious.

"Well, you know all that higher power bullshit they talk about in here? I don't call it that, I call it the universe. And it's kind of like that river, I guess. We can't see it from all the way back here, but we know it's there. We know it's busy doing what it does, whether we see it or not."

I leaned back in my chair and looked out to the treeline.

I didn't really know what I believed in, but what Silva said made sense.

Part of the treatment centre rules were to go to AA meetings and learn about recovery. I wasn't sure if I was really an addict or an alcoholic, but there seemed to be some sense of community here and in the meetings. And everyone seemed to be talking about believing in God or some other shit.

"So what do you think it means... the higher power stuff?"

"Well, maybe nothing.... But maybe something.... I guess we can just believe that maybe it's something or it's nothing."

Maybe nothing.

But maybe something, I thought back.

Maybe something.

"But I'll tell ya, if it's not the chicken quesadillas on the dinner menu tonight, I don't believe in it anymore," she chuckled, pulling her hand up to light a cigarette that was carefully dangling from her mouth.

I looked over to her, and as soon as our eyes met we both burst into warm and loud laughter.

"Ah, I'm just kidding, Hunnie. Whatever Darla makes is gonna be the best of the best. Just like home cooking."

Home.

I wondered when I would be going home.

Floor.

Tiles.

Cold.

Wake up.

The clock on the wall.

Look at the clock.

It's almost over.

Wake up

"Just go with it," he whispered as I shut my eyes tightly, no longer able to breathe.

Why can't I breathe?

WAKE UP.

My eyes opened.

32B.

The number on my nightstand was 32B.

I'm still here.

It was just a dream.

I pushed myself up, leaning my back into the headboard, trying to adjust my eyes to my surroundings.

Breathe.

It was just a dream.

Jenna, my roommate, lay peacefully across the room, obviously undisturbed.

I took a deep breath, grateful I hadn't woken her.

What time is it?

I didn't have a clock and our cellphones had been taken away the first night we arrived.

I scanned the room, searching for something to give me a clue about how long I had been sleeping.

And how long I may still need to lay here until wake-up calls began.

I wanted to get up and go out into the hallway.

There was a clock there just above the staircase that led down to the dining area.

I pulled my knees into my chest and rested my chin on them.

I realized then just how sweaty I was.

Go take a shower.

I had been taking two, sometimes three showers a day since coming here.

For the first few days I felt like I wanted to peel my skin off.

Every movement, every temperature felt uncomfortable.

Even the way the bed sheets felt on my skin made me feel strange.

And the burning sensation from the heat of the shower was the only thing that seemed to make it feel better.

In one of our therapy classes, the counsellor told us to try switching from a hot shower to a cold shower every two minutes; adjusting the temperature dramatically was said to be good for something.

I forgot what.

I tried to pay attention in the classes but often excused myself to go to the "bathroom."

I didn't usually make it to the bathroom but would instead go sit outside in the smoking area.

A couple of the other girls would join me and we would tell stories about our lives over the last few years.

There's was always much more dramatic than mine.

It's funny how you can meet someone in some random setting and not open up much to each other, but you meet someone in a place like this and you know their life story in a matter of minutes.

I liked it.

I liked the oversharing and the swearing and the crying and everyone just being so honest about how they felt.

It was refreshing.

As I sat on the bed, 32B, I thought about what we would be doing today.

Group therapy, circle time, arts and crafts, movie night.

Fuckin arts and crafts.

I may have been the youngest person here by almost a decade, but deep down all of us knew we loved arts and crafts.

We got to be kids again.

And I don't think many of the people here ever really had the chance to be kids.

Just then, I heard a loud knock on the main door to the house, which sat directly underneath our bedroom, followed by the sound of the door being opened.

Darla was here.

Darla arrived every morning at exactly 6:00 a.m. to begin cooking breakfast for all of us.

Go take a shower before the others wake up.

I slid myself as quietly as I could to the edge of the bed and leaned down into the little suitcase that lay open on the floor.

I collected a change of clothes and slowly crept towards the door, looking at Jenna while I did just in case she started to move.

I slid into the bathroom as quietly as I could, locking the door behind me.

I placed my bag of clothes and shower supplies on a small ledge beside the sink as I began to untangle my hair slowly, trying not to pull too harshly on the hair tie as I maneuvered it up, around and out of the tangled knot of strawberry blonde hair.

Finally, as it released, I watched in the mirror as it fell to my shoulders.

It was getting longer.

I ran my fingers through a mass of strands, separating them softly.

Silva was right.

I did look better.

The dark, sunken circles around my eyes had all but vanished. My eyes were bright, illuminated by the sea of freckles that washed over my face.

I had grown to like them.

When I was a little girl my grandmother used to tell me they were fairy kisses. And I believed her for longer than most children would.

I reached over to the ledge without looking to it to feel for my bag, which I promptly knocked over.

It fell to the floor, crashing down obnoxiously on the old white tiles.

I bent down quickly, grabbing at the scattered belongings, praying I hadn't woken everyone up.

I reached for a small shampoo bottle that had come out of the bag, grabbing it and placing it back inside.

As I did, I noticed a small white pocket knife tucked away absentmindedly at the very bottom of the bag, my name engraved on the back of it.

I wasn't sure how that had made it past the staff during inspection.

It was a gift from my father years ago, and something I had started carrying with me when I left home.

I liked to think it might make my father feel better to know that even though I wasn't there anymore, I was still trying to protect myself.

And in that moment, I wondered if he would be sad if he knew that I hadn't been able to use it that night.

That I couldn't protect myself.

I didn't know how to fight.

I didn't see myself as a very aggressive person; in fact, I would do almost anything to avoid a conflict.

Sometimes my dad would remind me that I wasn't always like that.

My mother called me her wild child, her free spirit.

I was alive.

Very much alive.

At some point.

I used to have this deep curiosity for life and wanted to experience as much as I could, all the time.

To the dismay of my very careful parents.

Somewhere along the line in these last few years, I felt that spark within me leave.

Slowly and then all at once.

I didn't know how to connect with myself anymore.

Suddenly the simpleness of life wasn't enough to sustain my curiosity any longer.

It felt childlike and I didn't want to be a child anymore.

I wanted to grow up.

And I didn't want to move anymore.

I wanted to be close to other people.

I wanted to hold onto friendships for years, like the way I had seen people do in movies.

Or the way I heard kids at school talk about their childhood friends.

To have someone know me, and learn me, and I could know them and learn them, and somehow we would just be running around exploring this life together.

I wanted friends.

I wanted to stop having to say goodbye to everyone.

But it's hard to do that when you move every two years.

And I was tired.

We all were.

Maybe it was the constant uprooting of our lives.

We began to pull apart from one another like the unwinding string of a sweater.

The tugging, aching, longing for a little bit of normalcy.

A little bit of stability.

Every new introduction seemed tiring and fake.

The people, the schools, the neighbourhoods, even the smells of our new surroundings.

It had been so fun when I was younger, but I didn't feel young anymore.

"Our next adventure!" my mother had exclaimed happily as she opened the door to our new home.

I dragged my feet through the entrance hoping — praying — that this was just a bad dream.

That I would wake up and be back in our old house, my old bed, my old purple room.

And which house was that?

I realized I was blending the memories of some of them together.

On that afternoon when we arrived in this city, my father had placed a hand gingerly on my back as we watched the old familiar moving truck puttering up the narrow cul-de-sac, announcing the arrival of our belongings.

"Have you picked your room yet?" he had said without looking at me but smiling sweetly the way he did.

I always knew if he was smiling by the sound of his voice.

What neither of us knew then was that soon enough there would be no need for a room for me there.

There was a war raging inside of him that I could see, ever so silently, beginning to come to the surface.

I wondered if he felt it then too.

It would be many years before the words post-traumatic stress would enter either of our vocabularies.

But on that sunny summer afternoon, I would pick my room. The one with the horrid pink pastels and poorly hand-painted flowers.

And on this sunny summer morning, I would get dressed and make my way downstairs, putting my last few worldly possessions away in my suitcase and locking the door behind me. 32B.

"I can't wait to get out of heeeeere!"

Jenna opened the screen door and burst outside, smiling from ear to ear.

"It's 7 a.m.," I laughed, sipping a cup of coffee as I pulled my knees to my chest.

The crisp morning air offering a reminder that summer would soon be coming to a close.

Jenna lit a cigarette, pacing excitedly from one end of the deck to another.

I didn't usually see her this cheerful in the morning, but then again, today was a day everyone was excited about.

Home.

We finally get to go home.

The house was alive this morning.

A bittersweet array of emotions as all sixteen of us grappled with the feelings that came with leaving this place.

A mix of excitement, fear, joy, sadness.

I wondered what everyone would be going back to.

Partners, children, jobs, their familiar routines, only this time with a hopeful promise that their yesterdays would be kept far behind them.

That sobriety was something tangible and even exciting.

I didn't hold the same hopes as the others.

It was hard for me to wrap my head around being an addict or an alcoholic. Especially at seventeen.

It felt too easy to simply say I was born this way and had some kind of illness. Maybe I did.

Maybe deep down, I desperately didn't want to think about letting go of the one coping skill I had left.

The one that worked.

Being here had felt like a pause in my previous activities.

A pause.

Not a stop.

And this would be the real test, the counsellor had told me.

The test of going back and sinking into my old life while trying to maintain some of the changes I had made here.

As I sat, thinking about what the rest of this day would hold, I heard the sound of a car pulling up to the front of the house. I suddenly realized we only had a few hours left together at most.

I looked down at the weathered spiral notebook that lay closed on my lap.

The edges delicately frayed with the wear of holding all of my deepest thoughts. All of my secrets.

It felt heavy to hold, but I felt empty without it.

I ran my fingers across the cover, touching my thumb to the edge to open it.

As I did this, I heard the old screen door open, and a voice spoke softly from behind it.

"Your parents are here," she said.

I looked up from my notebook to see the counsellor at the door staring at me.

The chatter around us began to quiet as the rest of the girls who had joined us outside looked to me.

The counsellor held my gaze gracefully, giving me a moment to pull myself together.

This was the test she was speaking of.

I had agreed to go home.

To try.

And in that very moment I wondered if I had made a mistake.

I wondered if I would be able to be the daughter they wanted.

If they would be able to be the parents I needed.

I didn't quite know how to explain it to anyone.

How could I be nervous to return to my biological home?

My family?

What was it about that place that made my skin crawl?

How could I simultaneously miss them but be terrified of going there?

But that's the thing.

You can miss something with every fibre of your being, and that still doesn't mean it's good for you.

Someone can love you with all that they are, but that doesn't mean that they will be able to guide you.

I so badly wanted to explain to them that I wasn't a bad kid.

I wasn't trying to make their lives harder.

It was hard enough already, I knew that.

I just wanted somewhere to feel like home.

And for whatever reason, I could never seem to find that.

I leaned my body into Jenna, who had taken a place neatly and supportively at my side, accepting the comfort and warmth that she would offer me in my last few moments there.

"It'll be okay," she whispered

"You'll be close to your friends again too."

My mind flashed back to our second week here when Jenna and I had been talking about where my parents lived and where some of my friends lived, not far from their house.

My stomach turned as my brain finally connected the piece I had been avoiding.

If I go back there… with them… I'll be very close to where he lives.

To where it happened.

And if I go back to the place I had been staying, I'd still be close by to where it happened.

Streets I would need to walk every day.

Bus routes that would pass by the same café no matter which route I needed to take.

All of them had to drive by there to get out of that part of the city.

I would be trapped.

There's nowhere you can go.

You have to leave the city.

How the fuck am I gonna do that? I thought back at myself.

But she was right.

"Are you ready?" the counsellor asked sweetly, drawing my attention back to her.

My parents were in the waiting area of the main house.

My suitcase had been packed and was sitting neatly at the front door along with the line of others. I'm sure my dad would be taking it to the car already, eager to see me and start our long drive back.

I took a deep breath as I stood up, pulling my sweater back over my shoulders. The other girls began to gather around me, some with tears in their eyes, all taking turns reaching out to embrace me, saying our final goodbyes.

Message Ray.

I brushed off this request.

We have such a long drive home, I could do it then, I told myself.

Fuckin message Ray, you need something ready for when you get there.

I am going to try and stay sober for a while, fuck off, I shot back at myself.

Goodluck with that.

You'll be driving by his house just to get home.

Please stop

Tiles.

Cold.

Floor.

Blood.

I'm doing better now.

I'm gonna do better, I pleaded with myself to stop as the memories and images flashed through my mind.

Let me be good right now.

Let me get through the next few months.

I can avoid people and places, I can get another job, I can switch schools, please just let me be for now.

You will not survive back there.

there are a thousand steps between who you want to be
and who you are
but only a few feet between where you've been
and the familiar war
and you fall back into darkness
because you say you can't find the light
or is it because you are tired of walking?
scared you will somehow run out of time?
push your heels into the pavement
broken heart and all
one step, two steps, three steps, four
over the ledge
let go and fall

— patterns

I stepped into the pristinely kept townhouse.

I always felt so awkward here.

It was clean and organized.

Every surface gleaming with the remnants of a recent polish.

My mother was quite like this too.

Everything in the house had its place, and every place was clean.

Take off your shoes, don' t talk too loudly, I would remind myself.

"Hurry up." Alex laughed, peering at me from the living room, sensing the carefulness in my steps.

"Come in, what do you wanna drink?"

I stepped through the hallway, minding myself as the noise and the people around me grew. I pushed past a few bodies, inching my way closer to him.

"Whatever you have," I yelled back.

I watched as he twirled around on a fancy black chair to face me.

The computer in front of him displayed a message box fresh with conversation from whoever he had been talking to.

He stood up and walked to the kitchen, tracing his hands over the several bottles that lay on the island in front of him, each one already open.

I immediately felt around to the back pocket of my jeans for my phone.

I must have left it at home.

I needed to tell Ray where I was.

I was supposed to meet her later.

My parents thought I was at her house at this very moment.

I had told them a story about having a sleepover.

Painting our nails and doing face masks. You know. Girly things.

Instead, I was here, two streets over, in a room full of people, about to down a few shots and see where the night took us.

"Can I go on?" I asked, motioning to the computer.

If I could at least sign into my account and message Ray, I could grab a bus and meet her somewhere later.

"Of course!"

Alex was always full of life. Full of excitement.

I sat down at the computer, letting my bag fall from my shoulder onto the ground as I began typing in my account details.

I logged in, scanning the active contacts for Ray.

She wasn't online.

I leaned back in the large and comfortable armchair as Alex came up beside me and placed a drink on the desk.

"I'm glad you're back," he said quietly.

Everyone had heard by now that I had gone to rehab.

"Glad to be back too," I said, looking up at him, smiling.

And I was.

Glad to be back.

The chaos of the last few months felt like it was slowly moving behind me.

Where it belonged.

Maybe I could start fresh here.

Get things right this time.

Alex placed a hand gently in between my shoulder blades, smiling to me.

His eyes quickly became distracted, looking to the computer screen.

"Someone wants to talk to you," he laughed, excusing himself.

A message had appeared on the chat box.
It was from Vee.
I froze.
I hadn't spoken to him in weeks. Since that awkward morning at his house.

Where are you?

I hesitated. I didn't want to do drugs tonight, and I knew if I spoke to him for too long our conversation may go there. I would end up asking.

At Alex's, I replied.

Oh so you're back now?

Yeah, got back last week.

Did you even go? To that treatment place?

I couldn't quite tell if he was being condescending or asking a question. I also didn't understand why he of all people really cared.

Yeah, I did. Why?

Just wondering. I heard you're a bit of a liar.

I sat very still for a moment, staring at the words displaying themselves crisply in front of me.
My fingers hovered over the keyboard.
I didn't know what to say.

I tried to think through past conversations.

I couldn't think of anything I had lied to him about.

Ever.

Our connection had never been deep or that concrete, but I hadn't lied.

I had accepted the fact that we didn't seem to mean much to each other, other than friends who sometimes stayed up later than they should.

And then I thought back to our last conversation.

The one where I told him I wasn't a virgin anymore.

You fuckin idiot.

He's talking to people about it.

She was right.

He was friends with people who knew him. People who were friends with him. Friends with me. Or used to be.

The conversation suddenly made sense to me.

He didn't think I was lying about going to a treatment centre.

Everyone knew I was there.

He thought I was lying about what had happened that night.

I felt my face begin to burn as I struggled to adjust my eyes to the words in front of me.

I looked around the room at the various faces. I went to school with some of them. I knew them. They knew me. Not far below the surface, but still. We would see each other in the hallways and hear about each other's lives. Vee was part of that. In some way. He had been a part of those conversations with me. And now, it seemed as though he was still very much a part of those conversations. Only now, I was the topic.

The runaway.

The liar.

I tried to piece together something to say.

It felt strange to write about something so personal in a message box on the computer.

Stand up for yourself.

She was firm. Confident.

I did not feel the same.

I really don't give a fuck what you think, I wrote, hesitating over the return button for a moment.

As I sat there, the anger building inside of me like a steady drip becoming a stream, I wondered how many people had been talking about what happened.

I thought back to everything over the last few months.

Every glance, every conversation, every slight remark or disregard.

How do you make people see your side of things?

You don't.

Some part of me knew she was right.

I looked at the drink sitting beside me. The one Alex had brought over.

I hadn't had one in a while.

That promise I had made to myself to abstain from everything.

The promise I made to my parents.

Are you sure you want to?

What else can I do? I questioned back to myself.

I need to forget about a few things.

That night.

Those friendships.

I would have felt better if people had just pretended it never happened.

And like I had imagined, the crippling anxiety began to build.

The feeling of knowing I was once again living in a place surrounded by people who knew something had happened.

People who knew one side of the story and aligned themselves with the one that made the most sense to them.

And your side will be forgotten.

I know.

I picked up the drink and brought it to my lips carelessly, taking the first sip and allowing the medicine to wash down my throat, taking pieces of my sadness with it.

And that was the purpose of it after all.

If I can't stop the fighting, the rage, the sickness that I felt inside the walls of my chest, I could certainly quiet it.

Couldn't I?

Just for a while.

I quickly pressed send and immediately logged off the computer.

I stood up and looked around the little townhouse which had filled up quickly in the few minutes I had been here.

Most of the people here didn't go to my school, but I began to recognize more of the faces. Out of the fifteen or sixteen people who had crowded into the house, all talking and laughing amongst themselves, I recognized three or four as people I had seen in classes.

I began to feel uncomfortable.

Paranoid.

I lifted my bag from the floor, searching inside for the pack of cigarettes I was sure I still had in there somewhere.

Found it.

I made my way towards the front door, pushing my feet into my shoes quickly as I opened the door to step outside.

Just go for a smoke, calm down and go back in.

I could do that.

I walked down the narrow pathway from the front of the house that led to the sidewalk.

It was quiet out here.

The streetlights were dimly illuminating the long row of identical townhouses that stretched out down the street, curving at the end and continuing on far beyond where I could see.

Suburbia.

I still wasn't quite used to it. Even after three years, I missed the wide-open fields and cozy military communities I was used to.

The rows of carelessly kept quarters, the neighbours that drank a bit too much, the other kids who were used to coming and going every year or two.

I missed all of it.

I constantly felt lost, but living on the military bases, you were surrounded by other kids who were just as lost. So you could be lost together. And you could be with people who understood your life.

Maybe that's what I was missing.

People who understood.

Or maybe it was me who just didn't understand.

As I looked down the darkened sidewalk and took a drag off my cigarette, I heard voices behind me.

I turned around, thinking people from the house were joining me outside, but the door to the house was closed, with only the dull echo of some heavy metal music rumbling through the cracks in the frame.

I looked down the sidewalk and saw four shadowy figures in the distance making their way towards me.

I stepped onto the grass, giving room for them to pass by.

As they grew closer, I recognized one of the girls. We weren't friends, but I had seen her many times. She had shown up at different parties or get-togethers I had been to.

She seemed confident but not in a way that made you feel comfortable.

She was aggressive, demanding attention and some kind of respect from those around her.

I wonder if she knew it wasn't really respect she was getting.

People were scared of her. Or maybe just scared to upset her.

I always found her difficult to read.

I think that sometimes when people are acting overly confident, deep down they are quite sad.

Maybe scared.

The group noticed me as they grew closer, the girl I recognized looked to me, glaring.

I knew it was a glare because it was too dark for it to be a squint.

I locked her gaze, obviously confused, but not wanting to back down.

If you look away in situations like this, you are conceding.

I was starting to feel a bit too tipsy to do that.

As the group moved past me, not slowing their pace, I heard the girl whisper loud enough for all of us to hear.

"Slut."

The word moved from her mouth, dropping into the air around us, hurling itself at my ears and into my chest.

The weight of it was stunning.

I looked to her, steps away from me now as she turned her head around to meet my gaze, offering a cruel smile before turning back and continuing on her way.

I could hear the others giggling.

Run.

My feet didn't move.

In that moment I wanted nothing more than to disappear.

To feel the concrete below swallow me up.

Hide me somewhere until this was over.

This rumour, this hollow knowledge that preserved the darkest moment of my still young life.

It was clear to me then what it had become.

A joke.

A trivial bit of information.

So what do you do when a piece of you is floating through the mouths of others?

Becoming a lie. A tale that gets spun in a hundred different directions but never landing on the truth.

Get the fuck out of here.

Where do we go?

Anywhere.

sometimes i cannot see the end or the beginning
fragmented pieces of everything i've done
everyone i've loved
circling the drain
and i wish i could blame it on you
i used to
but if it truly is your fault
do you fix it, or do i?
sometimes i cannot see the end or the beginning
just the same storm circling the drain
awaiting the rain

— the drain

The bus swerved in and out of the traffic around us, bouncing and swaying as it moved through the quiet residential neighbourhood.

The sun had begun to peek out of its hiding place beyond the clouds, scattering its warm reach in streams and patterns, flickering across the grass.

It was warm today.

Oddly warm for a November afternoon.

I hugged my bag to my chest as I slipped down farther into the cold metal bus seat. I didn't know where I was going today.

School had just finished, which left me the entire afternoon to find something to drink, something to eat and a place to sleep.

It had been weeks since I had seen anyone besides Ray and a couple of our mutual friends.

I couldn't bring myself to go to any of the same places for fear of running into someone.

Anyone.

On the odd chance that I would run into someone I knew, friend or foe, I was usually drunk.

Very drunk.

The first sober breath I would take in the morning was only enough to wake me up and begin my day of wandering through the city.

I went to the new school because they had a breakfast program, and I still needed to eat despite what my brain told me.

The counsellor there knew Nina well and would often usher me into her office to ask how I was doing and offer me gift cards to a local grocery store.

I quickly figured out how to use those cards to buy cigarettes, hence why I still showed up to school every morning.

Get another bottle and you'll be fine.

She would tell me every day.

And every day I would listen.

Because she and I both knew that any minute sober was a minute alone with my thoughts, and I couldn't do that right now.

Not anymore.

It was too hard.

I managed to get a new job in a grocery store across town, and although I was drunk for almost every shift, no one really seemed to notice.

Or maybe they did but thought better than to say anything.

The two or three shifts I worked each week were just enough to pay for my phone bill and keep me with decent cigarettes.

I rotated through different liquor stores around the west end of the city each afternoon.

I had figured out a certain section of the store that didn't have cameras.

I timed my visits around four or five o'clock each day.

The busier times, where I could go in relatively unnoticed, I could pretend to peruse the fine wine section while slipping a twenty-six-ounce bottle of vodka into my bag.

That would be enough to get me through the night and some of the next day.

On one particular afternoon, a man, maybe mid-forties was pushing a cart of alcohol out onto the storeroom floor preparing to re-stock the section I was coming out of.

I slid the bottle of vodka into my bag and rounded a corner to find him staring at me.

Fuck.

I figured at this point I had been caught, but I knew giving in meant it would be taken from me.

And I needed it.

I was starting to become quite sick without it.

The man paused what he was doing and looked at me from over the rim of his thinly-framed glasses.

He nodded to me before turning, picking up a case of beer and moving towards the aisle he was working in.

I let out a quick breath of relief before I picked up speed and walked quickly towards the exit.

Clinging to my bag tightly under my arm.

My small piece of relief.

Little did I know I would meet that man again in about three years' time in the basement of a church.

And he would embrace me warmly, looking over the rim of the same pair of glasses and offering me a cup of coffee and a ride home.

If only I knew then what my life would look like later.

The bus turned onto a familiar street, bustling along down the old road that led to my old high school.

My anxiety started to build as I realized where I was.

Too close.

Too close to everything and everyone.

I had gotten on the wrong bus.

I didn't want to come this way.

I shifted myself up in my seat, trying to find a landmark, somewhere I could get off quickly and redirect myself to another bus.

I tried to calm myself as the panic inside me began to take over.

Get off somewhere, anywhere.

Just start walking.

The bottle's almost empty, just find another route and get to a store.

I pulled the handle that rested against the bus window, signalling that I wanted to get off at the next stop.

As I did, I looked out the window and spotted a group of teenagers walking.

Four boys.

I knew them.

They had been there the night it happened.

The bus began to slow as I realized my stop was coming up.

Quickly.

The group was walking towards the old high school.

If I got off now, I could start walking the opposite direction and hope they wouldn't see me. I would be just far enough away.

My hands began to shake as I stood up, steadying my feet between the vigorous jolts of the bus as it slowed to a stop.

Tears were beginning to build behind my eyes, trying their best to leap forward as I fought with myself to calm down.

Don't be so fuckin dramatic.

You'll be fine, just get out of here and start walking.

I stepped off the bus and onto the pavement below, stumbling forward slightly.

I couldn't hold them back anymore.

The tears began to flow steadily, streaming down my face.

I cursed myself silently for being so fragile.

So weak.

Fuck you, I thought.

But not to myself this time.

To him.

Fuck you for doing this.

Fuck you for making me scared of my own neighbourhood, my own shadow.

Fuck you for lying, for taking my friends.

Just fuck you.

I stormed up the sidewalk, no longer caring who saw me, wiping tears away angrily as quickly as they came.

The bus moved past me, continuing on its route, and as it passed, I looked over across the street and saw a police station. It had been there for as long as I had lived here, but for some reason I hadn't really noticed it until now.

Maybe they can help.

Maybe you can tell them.

Report it.

Maybe they can do something.

I brushed off the idea.

It had been too long. Months.

If I was going to report anything it should have been that night, but that wasn't a thought that had even entered my mind at the time.

I stood for a moment, staring at the small brown building, and as if I was somehow watching my body outside of myself again, my feet began to move towards it.

Tell them.

I don't fuckin want to, I cried back, wiping another strand of salty tears from my face.

TELL THEM.

I crossed the street and approached the door to the station, my hand outstretched, hovering over the handle.

I thought about what this would mean.

Would they arrest him?

Would I have to go to court?

Would everyone hate me after this?

They already fuckin hate you.

It doesn't matter.

She was right.

Everyone already believes him. Maybe the police will believe you.

You have nothing left to lose.

I took a deep breath in.

Do it.

I pulled the door open, pushing myself into the station, hoping, praying that I wouldn't regret what I was about to do.

A man in uniform, maybe about fifty years old, stood behind a pane of Plexiglas.

I looked around, realizing I was the only one here.

Not too much business on a Tuesday afternoon in suburbia.

He looked at me, puzzled, as I stepped forward awkwardly, trying to think of something to say.

How do you begin a conversation like this?

"I need to report something," I said quietly, lacking confidence, as my mind finally realized what I had committed to.

The officer stood silently, surveying me, waiting for more information. He reached down in front of him and pulled up a clipboard.

Don't tell him. He's an old man, he won't fuckin help you.

Ask for a woman.

"I need to talk to a woman," I said, trying to sound more assertive.

The officer looked up from the clipboard, surveying me again, before letting out a long sigh.

Oh maybe that's too much work for him, my inner voice spat sarcastically.

He picked up a phone to his left and punched in a few numbers I couldn't see.

I didn't know who he was talking to, but as he spoke to them, he looked to me again.

"Maybe fifteen or sixteen," he muttered.

He put down the receiver, looked over to me and signalled for me to sit down in the line of cold metal chairs that sat empty beside me.

"Take a seat. It's gonna be a little while."

Oh fuck this.

We're here now, we may as well wait. The longer we stay inside, the less of a chance we have of running into anyone else, I thought.

I pulled out a pack of cigarettes from my bag, holding it in front of him and motioning outside.

He waved me off, which I took as allowance for me to wait outside.

Two hours went by as I sat on the curb of the crumbling sidewalk just outside of the station. The road that lay parallel to it was quiet and lacking the kind of traffic you get in other parts of the city.

I thought about where I would go after this.

I had been sleeping in various places over the past few weeks.

On one particularly cold night I had even broken into my parent's house just after midnight.

I had managed to get four or five hours of sleep before heading out early in the morning before they had woken up.

This was a task in itself, as my mother was always up before any sane human would be. And my father could spring from a deep sleep at the sound of a pin drop.

I thought better than to try that again.

Many nights I spent drinking and riding busses across the city. Sometimes I would fall asleep in bus shelters, but most of the time I tried my best to stay awake.

If I could stay awake during the night and then fall asleep at school or at Ray's boyfriend's house during the day, then I wasn't really homeless, right?

But the nights were getting much colder, and I knew I needed to find somewhere else to go.

Somewhere a bit more permanent.

I had seen Nina a couple of weeks ago, and she had mentioned going to another treatment centre. This one would be much longer than the first one, and I could even apply for some kind of shelter housing after.

I was almost eighteen.

I had told her I didn't want to go, and it was the first time I had ever seen her cry in one of our sessions.

She told me she knew I didn't want to go, but that she didn't think I would make it through the winter.

I was honest with her about how I had been living, and although I was fighting with everything in me not to be sent away again, I was coming to the fast conclusion that I had nowhere else to go.

And I certainly couldn't stay here anymore, in this city.

That was clear.

A cruiser pulled into a spot a couple spaces from where I was perched on the curb.

A female officer stepped out of the vehicle, locking eyes with me as she shut the cruiser door. She moved towards me slowly but with a gentle deliberation.

"Are you the one that called to do a report?" she said matter-of-factly, scanning my appearance.

The trails of tears that had previously lined my face were now just a memory as I sat, stone-faced, in my weathered jeans, a lopsided bag and an array of cigarette butts scattered at my feet. I was indeed the obvious candidate.

I nodded to her, swiping a tangled strand of unwashed hair from my eyes.

"There's a room inside we can go to. We'll be alone," she said softly, waiting for me to follow.

No turning back now.

Not like there ever was.

one day when you find the light inside of yourself
the one that had been so carelessly blown out
leaving a lonely trail of ashes and wax
when the waves have stopped
and you come up for air
grasping desperately at the shore
for all of the souls that didn't come for you
for all of the ones who wait to hear you
i hope you scream

— little secrets

Are you supposed to feel better?

When you tell someone the truth.

Something you hadn't wanted to say.

Something you needed to say.

Tell me, are you supposed to feel free?

The movies and TV shows will tell you that.

That once you come forward and bear your soul, you will cry and sob and there will be some kind of weight lifted from your chest.

A hope that some of kind of justice or vindication is near.

I wanted to believe that.

But right now it felt like someone had crept into my room in the middle of the night and stacked fifty solid bricks across my body, only when I woke up, I couldn't see them.

But I could feel them.

I could feel the weight, the pressure, and with it, the impossible task of just getting up, opening my eyes, leaning forward and knowing in that early morning moment that, although the bricks were still there, I had to get up.

And I had to carry them with me.

I hadn't yet learned how to take them off.

How to let them go.

So I clung to them.

Because although they weighed me down and I would surely continue to sink, they pressed against my body so firmly that without them, I was sure I would just float away.

And when you don't know how to tell people about the invisible bricks, you use them to build your walls instead.

And so I did.

One by one.

My anger. Brick.

My sadness. Brick.

My desperation. Brick.

My carelessness. Brick.

My sudden and complete disregard for the world around me.
Brick.

I rolled over on the thick black futon, opening my eyes and
realizing where I was. My sister's apartment.

I rubbed my eyes, pushing myself up, trying to piece together
how I had gotten here.

Flashes of the night before began entering my mind.

I had gone into a coffee shop sometime yesterday evening.

It was cold and I knew I could stay in there for at least a little
while.

I had recognized the man behind the counter, my sister's
husband.

I had known him for a long time, before they were even
married, but somehow had completely forgotten that he worked
there.

I didn't want him to see me looking the way I did.

Tired, drunk and lost.

I hadn't seen or spoken to my sister in so long.

To say we were estranged would be putting it lightly, but the
moment he saw me, he pulled out his cell phone, a mix of
eagerness and concern on his face.

He had asked if he could call my sister, and I had agreed.

I wasn't sure why.

I guess I figured if there was someone that would understand
part of what was happening, it would be her.

Within a few minutes of his call to her, she pulled up out front of the little coffee shop and rushed inside, searching through the oddly crowded space until our eyes met.

Seeing her, feeling her pull me close, made me realize at once how very dishevelled I must have looked.

She smelled like vanilla. Her clothes were clean, and her face looked bright and refreshed. She was older than me by a few years, but anyone looking at us that night would have surely guessed the opposite.

"You'll stay with us," she said, taking my hand, leading me out towards the car and away from whatever foolish thing I would have needed to do that night to stay awake.

Their apartment sat close to the big highway that led out of the suburbs and into the larger and more expansive part of the city. It was mere streets away from the area I was trying to avoid.

Not quite far enough away to feel safe, but far enough for now. And as the cold breeze of a nearing winter began to sweep its way across the city, I knew I needed to say yes.

I needed to have somewhere to go.

For now.

In the weeks that would follow, they would ask nothing of me. I would continue to drink, roaming the outer streets and downtown avenues, blacking out, getting arrested and coming to. And my sister would show up every time, gathering me from these tired streets, and bringing me back to the little apartment, the little black futon.

She didn't yell at me or tell me to leave.

She didn't even ask me to stop drinking.

Maybe she knew that wouldn't work.

I found it funny that this was the circumstance in which we were reunited.

After years of being apart, we were colliding with each other on completely opposing ends of the same spectrum.

She had come close to where I was right now.

Maybe that's why she didn't fight with me.

Maybe that's why she had taken my brother in as well for a short time a couple of years prior.

She understood.

The three of us, although so very distant, had all left the same house at different times, multiple times, for many of the same reasons.

She had left first, being the oldest, and worked to establish herself.

Always the overachiever, and it showed in her college grades and her ability to uproot herself quickly and confidently whenever she needed to change her life's direction.

I used to think she hated me, but I can see now she was scared for me.

People behave in all kinds of strange ways when they are scared.

I envied her for being able to move on with her life.

For being successful and recreating her entire existence.

I envied it because I wanted that too.

I wanted nothing more than to wake up and feel some kind of power.

Some kind of control over my emotions and my trajectory.

And I tried.

But the difference between her and I was that she saw her life in its entirety.

She looked to her future and made decisions that were hard to make now but would eventually lead her to where she wanted to be.

I looked at my life hours at a time.

The future scared me far more than the present.

And truth be told, if this was the way it was now, I wasn't sure if I wanted to stick around for the rest of it.

For the rising.

I would often hear people say that these young years of life were supposed to be the best.

They were supposed to be filled with adventure and excitement and the elusive process of finding yourself. Of seeing the brightness of your future.

So what do you do when the lights have gone out?

When your path isn't clear anymore and you can no longer see your reflection or your shadow?

And if I am truly just a poorly constructed puzzle. A collection of everyone I have known, how do I know which parts to hold onto and which to discard?

And maybe that's just the process of life.

Gathering pieces and holding each one, examining its contents and usefulness and deciding whether you should push it into your soul or let it go.

Because after all, new pieces will come, won't they?

I guess you just have to remain willing to look for them.

Les voies de fait contre un conjoint sont des crimes

La loi interdit les voies de fait, peu importe la relation entre la victime et l'agresseur. Vous ne méritez pas qu'on vous agresse. Ce n'est pas votre faute et vous n'êtes pas responsable des actes de votre partenaire. Rappelez-vous que la police et les organismes communautaires peuvent vous aider.

Signaler la violence à la police est une première étape qui aidera à prévenir d'autres épisodes de violence dans votre foyer. Il est important que vous sachiez qu'une fois que votre conjoint a été accusé, seul le bureau du procureur de la Couronne peut retirer l'accusation.

Une injonction, aussi appelée parfois « ordonnance de ne pas faire », est une ordonnance de la cour qui exige de l'agresseur qu'il cesse de vous molester, de vous importuner ou de vous harceler, vous et (ou) vos enfants. Une fois l'injonction émise, l'agresseur ne peut plus vivre chez vous.

Si vous changez d'adresse, dites-le à l'enquêteur chargé de votre dossier. Il pourra ainsi vous tenir au courant de l'évolution du dossier.

En plus de téléphoner à la police pour demander son aide et sa protection, vous pouvez demander à la cour d'émettre une injonction ou un engagement de garder la paix.

Pour obtenir une injonction en vertu de la *Loi sur le droit de la famille,* adressez-vous au Tribunal familial à juridiction regroupée / Cour supérieure

---

Violence conjugale
Fiche d'aide aux victimes

Cst. _____

Nom, matricule et unité de l'agent qui a répondu à l'appel

Enquêteur, section, n° de téléphone _____

N° du dossier _____

Case # C7-

Reported Nov 9 '01

ottawapolice.ca

look for your angels
in every storm you face
every darkened corner
and every lonely day
look for your angels

— *there is always someone*

The school was loud this morning.

Voices echoed through the hallways, bouncing off the creamy cement walls. Various swarms of teenagers were parading down the hallways, all moving towards their respective classrooms.

I walked behind a large group of kids who were going towards my class.

The Lifeskills class.

This was the entry-level requirement to come to this school.

Almost everyone started out in Lifeskills.

It was the "bird course."

The easiest one to pass, but the one that they required you be present each day for.

And in that sense, it was actually quite difficult.

I didn't know most of the kids here, however, we all seemed to have a general understanding of each other.

You don't end up at this school because things are going well.

I liked it here because I could come and go without any of the other kids really noticing.

I could fade into the background, comfortably left alone.

And the fact that I could eat breakfast here or take a nap added another level of comfort.

I could really be anonymous.

I liked the Lifeskills class because we talked about things that mattered much more to us than math equations we would never use again or art history.

We had discussions about life and emotions and our opinions on certain things. Important things.

The teacher was a tall, pristinely athletic man named Greg.

Another great thing about this school was that they insisted we call teachers by their first names.

No Mr. or Mrs. whatever.

I think this was a way for us to see each other as equals.

Greg would sit on the edge of a desk at the head of the classroom, greeting each student by name, offering a huge smile and asking each person questions about what they did that weekend or how their dog was doing.

He remembered things about each of us and obviously took a great deal of pride in being able to talk to us individually, trying and succeeding in developing some kind of trust.

There were only ten or fifteen kids in each class, another rule of the school, that made it much easier to keep track of us.

For the first few weeks, I sat at the very back of the classroom.

My hat tilted slightly lower than normal and my bag never leaving its trusted position at my shoulder.

I didn't wear hats, but lately it had become a much-needed accessory to not only hide my unkept hair but also to draw just enough of a shadow over my eyes that maybe, just maybe, he wouldn't be able to tell I had been drinking.

I tried to drink in the bathroom before the class started but would often need to excuse myself part-way through the class in order to sneak away and take another shot.

Just enough to keep myself from getting sick.

I thought I had been hiding it so well, until one afternoon Greg asked me to stay after the class had been dismissed.

We had spoken to each other many times before but always in passing.

A friendly hello or good morning followed a couple hours later with a goodbye and have a good afternoon.

I liked him.

I liked him because he didn't demand that I behave in a certain way in order to be there.

I just needed to be there.

I didn't have to participate in the discussions if I didn't want to, although he had a way of engaging each of us that made me feel like he was genuinely curious about what we had to say.

And when someone is really interested in what you say or what you think, it makes you want to talk to them.

I would watch his eyes light up when someone would start speaking, sharing about an idea or an experience.

He would sit quietly, letting his arms unfold and rest on either side of the desk he would be perched against.

His shoulders would ease and he would smile enthusiastically, urging whoever was speaking to go on, to expand on their idea.

He encouraged us.

On this particular afternoon I was low on my usual supply of vodka and it was starting to become obvious.

Only to me, I had thought.

My hands were shaking more than usual, and my skin felt as if it had a layer of dampness to it, even in the cold.

I felt sick.

I watched as the rest of the students began filing out of the classroom.

I sat with my arms folded across my chest, holding myself tightly and wondering what he could possibly want to talk to me about.

As the last student shuffled out of the room, he looked over to me, the smile slowly fading from his face as a look I had seen before started to emerge in its place.

Concern.

"I read your paper," he said quietly, as he stood up from behind his desk and made his way closer to me.

He pulled a chair over to where I was sitting, placing it a few feet across from me before sitting down and once again letting his arms fall down beside him, resting his hands openly on his lap.

Looking to me and saying without words, I'm here.

"You have a gift," he continued, that big bright smile returning.

"Thank you," I nodded.

I thought about the paper I had written last week.

He would often give us a topic to discuss and would sometimes ask us to write something about it.

A paper, an essay of some sort.

He didn't usually label the assignment, but I knew what it meant.

I had been writing ever since I could remember.

Stories, poems, songs, whatever came to my mind or whatever I was experiencing at the time.

More recently it had become harder for me to write about life as I was living it. My deepest thoughts would come out in long drawn-out poems that usually didn't make any sense because I was too drunk to form a properly worded thought.

But this assignment, this paper, made me focus on something.

It made me question a lot of things.

He had asked us to write about our families.

More specifically, to write about what family meant to us.

I don't know what came over me during that time, as this wasn't information I was willingly sharing with anyone except Nina, but when I picked up the pen and began to write about it, about my family, something inside of me simultaneously broke and snapped into place.

Maybe I was starting to understand why I had been so sad the last few years. Maybe I knew deep down that he would read it and he would care.

Even if it never turned into an after-school conversation, he would sit at his desk or his dining table at home and he would read my words and he would give a shit.

"I don't know exactly what you're going through right now, but I just want you to know that you're not alone."

He leaned forward slightly in his seat, looking to me, drawing his gaze under the brim of my hat and seeing my face.

My bloodshot eyes.

My sadness.

I knew in that moment that he was looking at me.

Really looking at me.

In a way that nobody had in so long.

Or maybe they had but I just wasn't looking back.

"If you want to talk, or hell, even if you don't wanna talk and just need to sit with someone, I'm here. We are all here."

This wasn't the first time someone had said this to me, but for some reason, on that cloudy afternoon, I heard him.

It's funny how sometimes we can hear the same thing many times, but one day, out of the blue, we hear it in such a way that it sifts past all the layers we had built up in front of it and hits a part of ourselves that we forgot needed to be seen. A part that needed the light when we had kept it in the shadows for so long.

I wanted to cherish that moment.

I wanted nothing more than to sit with him and talk about how afraid I was and how I was watching myself fall apart and I just needed someone to sit with me while I put it back together.

I wanted to cry and scream and have someone witness this pain.

Please tell me it's not all for nothing.

Please tell me I'm not crazy.

Please, just please fuckin tell me it's going to be okay.

I'm going to come out of the other side of this.

I'm going to get through it.

And lie to me if you must, but please help me believe there is something better than right now.

That there is life after all this.

But I didn't do that.

I looked at him and I thanked him for being so kind and I made up an excuse about having to leave early to catch the next bus.

He was gracious and sweet and told me to tell him if I needed anything.

As I stood up and collected my things, placing them in my bag and making my way to the door, what he would say next would change everything about that day. It changed the way I was thinking about things in that moment.

Like an angel coming down from the sky and gently placing a path in front of me. And the funny thing was that it wasn't even that profound.

I reached out for the door handle to begin my walk to the bus stop when he called out to me, quietly, still sitting in the same chair close to my now vacant desk.

"You can keep going without them, you know?"

This caught my attention.

I turned to look at him, listening carefully.

"I know you think this is it, but it's not. There's a whole other life waiting for you. A better one... you can keep going."

That could be true, couldn't it?

Maybe there is a version of me out there, ten years from now, that will look back on this memory.

Maybe older me would be sad that we felt like we couldn't keep going.

Maybe older me would show me the life we built after all this... the one I almost missed.

The one that is good.

Could it be that there are just so many chapters untouched and unwritten?

Maybe he's right.

Yes.

Maybe he's right.

oh, little girl
how i have cried for you
in your sorrow and in your joy
in your wandering of all these places
sit with me for a while
and maybe when we are old and grey
sitting on the front porch of some weathered old house
we will cry about these days
i hope so
and in the middle of your best afternoon
when you are dancing in your kitchen or illuminating rooms
i hope you remember the things we've seen
i hope you will come back for me

— the other side

I stepped into the bus and looked past the few people hovering in front of me to peak above their heads to see the driver.

It wasn't Mark.

I pushed myself past the line of other teenagers standing amongst each other, crowding the already limited space we had.

I spotted an empty seat by a window about halfway down the length of the bus. This was rare at this time of day.

I moved past a few other bodies, pushed my way over to the vacant seat and plunked myself down, releasing my bag from my shoulder and placing it onto my lap.

Today had been better.

I managed to stay sober this morning and had finished all of the assignments Greg asked us to complete. I was even working on an extra essay to be considered for the school newspaper.

Greg thought I was a good enough writer that I should submit some of my work to various places.

He suggested starting small first and then working my way up.

A school newspaper seemed like a good enough place to start.

It had been a long time since I had felt any purpose in my schoolwork.

I remembered the old high school and all the hours spent trying to memorize equations or theories.

What a fuckin nightmare.

I was glad to be away from there.

For a lot of reasons.

I pulled my bag closer to me and opened it to search for my music player.

The CD player I had was old and skipped if I held it at a certain angle, which wasn't always conducive to my lifestyle.

As I reached into my bag and tried to untangle the nest of wires my headphones had created, I heard a muffled ringing.

My phone.

I reached farther into my bag to feel for my cell phone, which was vibrating frantically.

I looked at the number displayed on the screen.

I didn't recognize it.

I hesitated for a moment, wondering who would be bothering to call me in the middle of the day.

Maybe it was my brother.

He would sometimes call from different numbers.

I answered, holding it up to my ear.

"Hello?"

A female voice introduced herself on the other end.

It was the police.

An investigator.

"I've been assigned to your case."

I sat frozen as the bus rolled away from the busy intersection just outside of the school.

I wasn't sure what to say.

"Do you have anything from the night that it happened?" she pressed. "Your clothes, maybe?"

They want evidence.

I thought back to the morning after it had happened.

How I had peeled off my clothing, shaking violently as I grabbed at the shorts and T-shirt and hastily threw them into a garbage bag.

I didn't want to see them ever again.

I wanted to be rid of any reminders of that night.

"No," I said quietly, holding the phone closer to my ear and sinking down into the harsh metal seat.

I didn't want anyone around me to hear this conversation.

There was a long pause, then the investigator let out a sigh on the other end of the phone line.

This obviously wasn't what she wanted to hear.

"Given the, uh, length of time and the lack of physical evidence, I… pressing charges wouldn't be possible but… we can talk to him if you want?"

Talk to him?

You can talk to him?

And say what? Tell him to be a good boy from now on?

If she talks to him, he will know you said something.

"I don't… I don't think that will help," I said, my voice breaking with the realization that I had told them all of this for nothing.

The thinly-framed hope I had clung to without even realizing it.

The hope that someone would do something.

The hope that someone who was supposed to do something would do something. But what is this now?

"If you change your mind, just let me know."

Fuck you.

I hung up the phone, quickly pushing it back into my bag.

Well, there you go.

Stop it.

You wanted so badly to tell someone, and just fuckin look at what happened? NOTHING.

Please stop.

Tiles.

Cold.

Floor.

Blood.

I don't want to think about this anymore.

So don't.

Pretend it never happened.

I can't just turn it off and on like that; that's not how memories work, I spat back to myself.

If they can do it, so can you, she seethed.

Do you really think anyone cares about this?

Stupid girl.

You're just another slut who drank a bit too much and couldn't keep herself under control.

Stop it, that's not what happened.

Maybe it is.

Maybe it has to be.

But that's not what happened.

And where has the truth gotten you, huh?

It never fuckin happened.

See?

See how easy that was?

Say it.

It's not true, I inhaled sharply trying to catch my breath.

Then make your own reality.

Cuz you're not doing so hot in this one.

And just like a light had been turned on in a forever darkened room, I saw a way out… for now.

The only life I had known here, the only friends I had made, the only places I had stayed, all being ripped out of my hands in this silent wave of chaos.

Nowhere felt safe anymore.

And if the people around me don't believe me, and the police can't help me, what do I do now?

Pretend it never happened.

Fine.

It's 12:30 am ... so technically the 3rd
██████ I miss everything I used to
be. I've lost all hope. I've lost
everything. Hello? Hello? Hello,
now that everything is unclear, I'm
feeling so alone. No matter how close
people seem to be, I always end up on
my own.

— bye

you don't touch me anymore
but your hands are still wrapped around my throat
gripping and clawing
taking the very last breath for yourself
you don't speak to me anymore
but your voice is eating its way through my ears
shifting and pouring into my lungs
you don't recognize me anymore
and that's why I am coming back to find you
because if I am falling off this ledge
you're coming down with me too

— *tick tock*

"I kept your name on the waiting list."

Is she allowed to do that?

"Are you allowed to do that?" I asked casually, not truly wanting to know the answer.

I knew she probably already had to get some kind of approval to keep working with me.

I was certainly so far away from the general criteria now.

I had told her weeks ago that I didn't want to go away again.

To another facility.

I didn't feel like I was ready.

Quietly hoping the storm would pass on its own.

In time.

Nina reached out to me, ignoring my question and holding out a blank piece of paper.

"We should make a list of what you will need. When you get the phone call, you'll need to check in right away. You'll be there for four months."

What the fuck?

She hadn't told me that until now.

I leaned forward, slowly taking the piece of paper from her and placing it on top of my notebook that had been resting in my lap.

Where it usually was.

I stared at the floor, trying to think of something to say.

An excuse maybe.

Searching my brain for some kind of reason why I shouldn't go.

Maybe if I could just move to a different part of the city and start over, a new school, new surroundings.

Maybe I could get a grip on myself.

Her office was dark.

I think she kept it that way on purpose sometimes. The dim lighting and lack of windows somehow made me feel more comfortable. And plants.

She always had a couple of plants that clearly didn't require any sunlight to survive.

She had told me years ago that being around plants actually makes people feel more settled.

The little tricks you think of when you're caring for people who never seem to be very settled.

"What if I just get a different job?" I said quickly, clinging to my weak reasoning.

Nina sighed and looked at me defeatedly.

"I could get more hours somewhere else. I could start making enough money to live on my own or maybe move to that youth shelter. I could—"

She raised her hand into the open space between us, closing her eyes for a moment, signalling for me to stop.

I went quiet.

Fiddling with the pen in my hands, suddenly empty of words.

Empty of excuses.

Just empty.

I wanted to leave this place. I did.

I couldn't picture my life here anymore.

Not the way it was now.

But I didn't want to live in a centre again.

Surrounded by other unruly teenagers.

Being told when I could sleep, when I could eat, when I could pee.

It seemed too intense, too dramatic.

Maybe we were overreacting?

"I met you when you were fourteen."

I looked up at her.

Her eyes displayed a certain sadness I wasn't used to seeing.

Our sessions were usually filled with her listening intently to my ramblings, followed by an optimistic curiosity about what the future could hold.

What my future could hold.

Lately, we didn't talk about the future as much.

She knew she couldn't bring me to that place anymore.

Anything beyond the next few hours or few days and I would lose focus.

Lose hope.

I was tired.

Like I had been running through some kind of deep dark forest, constantly looking for the path only to be swallowed up again amongst the trees. And she was tired too.

I could see that now.

"I have been watching you trying to come through all of this. And you've tried. Very hard. I know that." Her sincerity was firm.

She dropped her gaze from me to the floor, somehow struggling with what she was about to say next.

"If you don't go to this place, I'm not sure what else I can do for you. I won't be able to keep working with you."

As her words floated into my ears and sunk down deep into my chest, I felt as if I could hear a little piece of my heart breaking.

It hurt her to say this.

It hurt me to hear it.

Nina had been a calming force for me over these last few years.

And the thought of not having her in my life was immediately terrifying.

Who would I talk to?

Ray and I were drifting further apart the more I isolated myself.

My sister clearly knew I was struggling, but I tried to spare her from all of the details, from the truth.

Nina was the only one who had seen me from the beginning of all of this.

And she stayed.

Maybe you should go.

I'm scared, I thought to myself.

I know.

But aren't you scared now? Being here?

I am.

Then maybe it wouldn't be so bad being scared somewhere else?

I don't know if I'm ready for this.

What if there really is another life for you?

After all of this?

And I thought about life.

I thought about what Greg had said that afternoon.

What if I live through this and there is something else, something better waiting for me?

A tear made its way past my eyes and treaded carefully down my cheek.

I looked to the piece of paper in front of me, cradling the pen in my left hand as I thought about the next chapter of my life.

I brought my hand, slightly unwillingly to the top of the page.

"Socks," I wrote.

Nina looked at me, her shoulders relaxing as she watched me begin to write my list.

Socks, I thought.

I would probably need those.

i looked up at the clouds with you that day
tracing the linings with our eyes
making shapes and promises
and you had asked me to stay
hoping that i was the same girl you had met before those days
that my smile would return
that my eyes would come alive
teach me how to be brave
i whispered quietly, just for us
and you would get up and leave that day
owing me nothing
but setting the stage

— curtains

"You're the new girl?"

I looked up from my bed where I had been sitting cross-legged, unpacking some of my things, to see a girl peeking her head around the doorway.

Her jet-black hair fell just past her shoulders and swayed gingerly as she tilted her head to the side, surveying me, smiling. She was tall.

I couldn't quite tell if she was a counsellor, although she didn't look old enough to be a staff member.

"Yeah, just got here today." I stopped unpacking and held my hands still for a moment, not wanting her to think I wasn't paying attention.

"My name's Darcy," she announced, smiling enthusiastically. "See you downstairs in a few?"

"For... what?" I asked hesitantly.

"We have group in ten minutes. You'll meet everyone else then too," she smiled.

And as quickly as she had appeared, Darcy swung around and made her way down the steps and back down into the main house.

I had forgotten what treatment was like.

Group therapy, AA meetings, crafting circles, chores. And I had heard someone say something about a weekly gym trip.

On the way in I had spotted a large white van sitting beside a line of about three or four cars in the oversized gravel driveway out front, and if you looked towards the grass just beyond that you would see... well, nothing else of interest. Miles of rolling fields surrounded the big brick house, which sat pleasantly amidst the country terrain.

"See you in a few months," my sister had said just hours before, tears streaming down her face as she was ushered away from me. Handing me over to a group of strangers who were charged with the task of "fixing" me.

Fixing us.

I heard a bell ring from the floor below me.

The sound was like an old cattle bell you would hear in some lowly farmer's field signalling it was time for us to gather.

A slow and steady rush of footsteps began from the hallway outside of my room.

Time to join them.

I slid my bags away from me, hopped off the bed and made my way towards the door.

Group.

I wondered what we would be doing there.

I wondered how many people were here.

When I arrived, the staff began their intake duties, closing several doors on the main floor that connected to other areas of the house.

I guess they didn't want the rest of the group seeing me just yet.

I was grateful for that.

I already had enough anxiety simply being here.

I sauntered down the stairs that led down to the main house, turning a corner to see a man with a clipboard standing stone-faced in the little hallway that led into a larger portion of the house I hadn't seen yet.

He peered up from the clipboard, staring at me.

"You're late" he said coolly.

"The bell just rang," I shot back, obviously confused.

"You're new. You should have reported down here ten minutes ago."

I had a vague recollection of one of the other staff members telling me that a couple of hours ago, just before I was taken upstairs to have my bags searched. Because they do that here. Apparently, more people than you would think try to sneak drugs into rehab.

"If you're going to do well here, you're going to need to follow the rules, and the first one is be on time."

Well, excuse me.

"Sorry," I muttered, realizing this wasn't a fight I wanted to have.

Nor was it one I was going to win.

He nodded to me, motioning down the previously closed hallway.

"After you," he said, the coldness in his tone receding.

brainwashed. Fuck. anyways I dont
have a roommate, which is good cuz
I'm crying.

Day 2 Jan 4th, 08
not much is happening. We had breakfast
and now ~~we~~ I'm watching people play
this guessing game. I wish I had
more confidence. Shit. Its just after 10 am
I did all my paperwork this morning.
I played guitar a bit yesterday. It was
good to do something I actually love. I'm
starting to remember how important the
little things are Oh! and I went to the
office and got my lucky penny back

There were twelve of us. All ranging in age from sixteen to twenty-one, and all coming from various parts of the province. The large brick house was divided into two sections, with the main common area and dining room centred on the main floor. The east side of the house was for the boys, and the south side was for the girls.

I heard chatter about how some of the boys would try to sneak onto the girls' side during the night.

I guess this was true, as the staff had installed a motion sensor on one of the staircases on the east side of the house, which connected to our side.

It was forbidden for any of us to use that staircase.

One of the staff members demonstrated for us. He walked out of the main common room and turned a corner to head up the east staircase. As he did, an alarm sounded, as promised.

I allowed myself to sink deeper into the tattered plaid loveseat as the staff member who had so warmly greeted me moments earlier introduced me to the group.

"Would you like to tell us a bit about yourself?" he asked warmly, a friendlier disposition than earlier.

I felt like fresh meat as I looked up to see the eyes of those around me hovering over my appearance.

I didn't feel much like myself.

I didn't look much like myself either.

My hair was shorter than I usually kept it and had been dyed an awful deep brown, illuminating my pale complexion.

I thought back to that night at my sister's apartment when I had taken the kitchen scissors to my once long and beautiful strawberry locks, cutting them to my shoulders before deepening them with a horrible box dye that was actually supposed to be black.

My hair had rejected it slightly that night, almost as much as I did now.

When you're drunk most of the time, you always think you look a little better than you actually do.

I had been sober for twelve hours now and had begun to notice just how much I had neglected myself.

And just how uncomfortable I was at every waking moment.

I tried to relax my shoulders to appear more confident as I told the group my name.

It felt weird to hear myself say that out loud.

My own name.

I scanned some of the faces in the room, and they all took turns nodding slightly and offering smiles, waiting for me to continue.

To offer up something else that would explain just a little more about who I was.

And who is that?

In that moment I wanted to run.

I wanted to jump off this couch and run.

Out the door, down the narrow gravel road, out into the fields, anywhere.

Just get me the fuck out of here.

The counsellor began speaking again, explaining some of the activities we would be doing today and going over the house rules.

More for my benefit that anyone else's.

I hadn't quite noticed until that moment just how many windows were surrounding us.

The winter sunlight beamed from across the fields around us, bouncing off of the snowy hill tops and climbing its way through the old country windows.

It was quite pretty out there, I thought to myself as my attention shifted from whatever the counsellor was saying.

I looked out a large, long window that sat across from me.

You're far away from all of that now.

This was the first calming thought I'd had since coming here.

I was far away from all of it.

For now.

But what if this doesn't work?

What if I have to go back there and nothing changes and I have to live there again and see those people?

What if I can't do it?

But what if you can?

3²⁹ pm - I feel like shit. I wanna cry /scream/die. I dont know whats going on. We got a new girl, I worked out at the gym, I got my 3 week review and that was okay. I cant take compliments very well. I wanna go home but I know that wont be okay. If I leave now I'll die but I feel like I wanna die now. ▮▮▮▮ came into the back room after I put out snack and was like 'Hayley' I said 'what?' and she just shook her head and kinda smiled. I wanted to kick her in the face. I'm annoyed, angry, upset. I feel like I cant talk to anyone. Shutting down once more. And I'm not even going to ask why ▮▮▮▮ cant love me,

Day 23 Jan 25th, 2008

9:06am - Not much is going on. Just finished chores. I was washing dishes and ███████ came in to get some water and then she started puking into the garbage. I asked if she was okay but thats sort of a dumb question to ask when someones withdrawling off heroine. She seems so nice though, I hope she stays. I sent ████████ back a letter this morning and I'm gonna start drawing/ making cologes?^ more and send them to her and my brother. Yesterday I was really homesick and I started crying when I talked to ██████ and I realized something today. Feeling like that here is a good thing because I can get through it without using and wake up feeling grateful. I dont really get these spells of depression and comedowns too much anymore. ████████ to be okay but then its like this huge

It's 2:00 a.m. I can hear a slow and methodic moaning coming from the room across the hall.

Not the kind of sound you would hear from pleasure, but one of immeasurable pain.

A sickness, I heard one of the staff call it.

Veda was in that room, and she was alone.

She had arrived two days ago from one of the larger cities west of here.

The only girl on our floor who had a room to herself.

And now I kind of understood why.

I sat up in my bed, my eyes trying their best to adjust to the darkness.

I looked over to see my roommate Lyla sleeping peacefully across the room.

I thought about going to Veda to see if she was okay.

I had heard her throwing up in the downstairs bathroom earlier yesterday afternoon.

I was completing my daily chores, emptying the garbage cans on the main floor and making my way to the larger bathroom on the south side of the house. The one that most of us never used.

As I walked down the hallway and closer to the bathroom, I heard the familiar gagging.

I stopped, not sure if I should wait there or quickly leave the area. Veda opened the bathroom door and emerged into the hallway.

She looked up to me as we both stood at a kind of standstill in the darkened hallway.

She had dreadlocks that reached down far past her shoulders.

She was thin — very thin — and her eyes displayed a sort of cloudy indifference.

I felt as if she was looking straight through me.

She said nothing as she broke my gaze absentmindedly, sauntering past me down the hallway.

Once she was far enough out of sight, I wandered into the bathroom to complete my chores.

The garbage can was sitting beside the unclosed toilet, which held the splatter of Veda's freshly ejected bile.

I tried to ignore it, leaning down to pick up the garbage can, and as I did, I noticed the tiles below.

They looked familiar.

I had seen that colour and that pattern before.

Cold.

Blood.

Floor.

Tiles.

The small garbage can slipped from my hand and tumbled to the floor as I stepped back suddenly. Those familiar images I could never seem to remove from my mind, drifting in once again.

No, I had thought to myself.

We won't be thinking about that anymore.

I straightened my back and relaxed my shoulders as I leaned down again, grabbing the garbage bin and emptying its contents into the large black bag in my other hand.

I sat up in my bed thinking about my encounter with Veda at the bathroom when I heard a soft restless sigh.

It was Lyla, who was now wide awake, pushing herself up in her bed and looking over to me.

Veda's soft and hopeless groans could still be heard from across the hall. She was desperate for relief from whatever chemicals were making their way out of her body.

"Again?" Lyla huffed, rubbing her eyes.

"Must be pretty bad," I said, acknowledging Veda's obvious overwhelming plight. I had never done heroine before.

There were a few of us here who had spared ourselves the dilemma of opiate addiction, by choice or by chance, I wasn't really sure.

"Darcy's leaving today," Lyla announced, peering at the far wall to the calendar that had been taped up a few weeks ago.

She was right.

Today's date had a red heart on it with a little sad face drawn underneath it.

I had drawn it on there to mark both the celebration and the sadness.

It was something each of us looked forward to, and the staff made sure to make a really big deal about it.

It was a celebration when one of us completed the program and finally got to go home.

Darcy and I had become very close recently. The thought of her not being here anymore was lonely, although I was happy for her.

Really happy.

She had been accepted into one of the girls' shelters right in the heart of the city. The staff had suggested I go there as well when I get out of here.

It was exciting to think Darcy and I might be able to live together again after all this.

Out in the real world.

I wondered what life would be like after all this.

As I looked at the calendar, it dawned on me that I had been here for two months. It felt like much longer.

My hair had started to grow, and the awful dark auburn hue was beginning to fade. My skin was clear and much brighter than it had ever been before. I carried my black coil notebook with me everywhere, writing several times a day about everything we were up to here. All the comings and goings of new and departing kids, and whatever goals we had set to work on for that week. There were about ten staff members that rotated through the house on either daytime or overnight shifts. Each one had a unique personality that evoked their unique skill set, and each one of them made sure they spent time with each of us over the course of their shifts. Guiding us through group counselling sessions, leading us through house chores, or setting up card games and other activities on the rare time that wasn't diligently scheduled. They kept us on a strict routine for the most part. Each morning we would wake up and gather down in the main common area, setting up the dining room for breakfast. We recited the twelve steps of Alcoholics Anonymous before each meal. Something that was slowly being drilled into us. The idea that we were all addicts and alcoholics and needed to admit our defeat and powerlessness over our former lifestyles. This was a necessary step, they would tell us. A crucial first step in moving towards freedom from our uncontrollable urges to drink or do coke, and to prevent us from lighting that destructive torch under our families and friends. I wasn't sure if this was true. I was merely seventeen after all. Was all of this happening because I had been born with this insidious illness that I could never be free from? Over the last few weeks

I had grown tired of fighting the concept. Maybe they were right. Maybe I did just need to surrender myself to a life of abstinence and recovery in order to get better. A few days ago over breakfast, one of the counsellors was sitting next to me, surveying us quietly as we took turns reading the steps out loud before lunch. I looked to him and he looked over, meeting my gaze, seeing my curiosity. I leaned over to him.

"Do you think we're really all addicts?" I asked, genuinely. I had grown to quite like and respect this counsellor, and I valued whatever answer he was about to give.

"Well," he paused, contemplating my question without breaking my gaze. "I think that it doesn't really matter what brought you here. You couldn't continue living the life you were living out there. You needed to surrender to something to get better.... I guess you could always go back to what you were doing before when you leave."

Although he hadn't answered my question, the last part of his statement sent a shiver from the base of my neck that carefully glided down my spine. How I had been living just before coming here wasn't something I wanted to go back to.

As the chatter and laughter erupted around us, signalling that the prayers had ended and the meal was now beginning, I decided in that moment that whether it was true or not — about me being an addict — I needed to stay here. I needed to do whatever they told me, and I needed to find a way to survive after all this. As much as I loved my sister and brother-in-law and wanted to be able to go back there and start my life over, something inside of me doubted whether I could return to that apartment. To that little suburban landscape that had been so suddenly tainted in the few months prior. I hadn't been able to take a breath in that place without it being immediately followed by a bottle of vodka. And if I couldn't go back there, I would need to move into one of the shelters. The thought of living in a shelter didn't scare me. But the thought of trying to survive there while drinking the way I had been did.

Maybe I didn't have all of the answers now, but this surely could be one of them, couldn't it? I had been treading, with very little care, along this invisible line between survival and living. Between life and death. Maybe if I just held on for a little longer and took someone else's advice things would get better? And maybe that's what surrender looks like sometimes. Acknowledging that, in this moment, someone else seemed to know what to do a little better than I did.

As I sat at the head of my bed thinking about all of this, I listened to Veda's soft and desperate moans from across the hall. I looked over to Lyla, who was now wide awake and sitting at the head of her bed as well, staring off into the space around us.

We would be okay, wouldn't we?

q55 - Today was alright - almost 70 days clear. I miss Mom. I just started thinking about her and I wonder what shes doing, if shes okay. I hope she can be happy one day. I hate thinking about these things cuz its so sad.

March 11th/08   Day 69

"How about we all start by making a list of the things that addiction has taken from us?"

Vikki looked to be about thirty years old.

She was tall and slim and was one of the only counsellors here who smoked, although she would do it in the parking lot just before coming in for her shift.

I would see her out there sometimes, a slight tinge of jealousy as I watched her take one haul after another off a king size Belmont.

We all had to quit smoking within the first few weeks of coming here.

"I want you to think about what life was like for you when you were using."

I glanced around the room, watching as the faces around me quieted their personal conversations, the laughing and smiles dimming from their banter as they thought about what she was asking.

"Think about what's been taken from you… what you've missed out on… maybe who you've missed being with. And just shout it out."

Vikki steadied herself, a bright blue marker in hand hovering over the blank page.

The room was quiet with contemplation.

"Graduation," a voice spoke from the couch beside me, breaking our silence.

"My brother's wedding," another shouted.

"The birth of my daughter."

"My dad's funeral."

"Being a good daughter."

The answers were coming faster now as Vikki kept up, frantically writing our secrets onto the page.

"Being able to see my sisters."

"Keeping a job."

"Having a place to live."

"Being happy."

I thought about that last statement as the voices around me began to drift out of tune.

What does it mean to be happy?

How will we know once we get there?

This seemingly unattainable moment when our struggles collide with our resiliency and we awaken a force within ourselves to carry on.

Is that what happens?

Will we each wake up one morning ten years from now, complaining half-heartedly about the business of our awaiting work day, greeting the early morning sunrise, making coffee and maybe even shuffling kids off to school?

Coffee is fuckin gross.

I know, I replied to myself.

I think that sometimes the purpose of life isn't really happiness at all but just purpose itself.

Some kind of direction.

Something that makes you feel like you are moving forward.

And maybe it wouldn't be such a bad thing to want the boring job and nights spent beside someone I love.

It seems like such an easy thing to write on paper, but when you are seventeen and in your second facility (with two more to come), it feels like you are standing at the bottom of the highest mountain.

And this mountain reaches so far into the clouds that you cannot see its peak. You have no way of knowing how long it will take you to climb it or if what you are looking for is even up there. But something inside of you knows that the paths at your feet have not been able to lead you anywhere worth going.

And so what do you do here?

You start climbing, I suppose.

Is that what I'm doing here... climbing?

I hope so.

what if I told you that there is no happy ending

would you stop listening?

would you run?

or worse, would you cover your ears with your worn and beaten hands

and pretend you didn't hear?

i hope so

and when i tell you there is no happy ending

it's simply because there is no ending at all

you and i will float through both time and space

colliding with each other in every lifetime

and we will reach for one another

never touching

as our souls cry out for what is lost again

and our angels will scream they are doing what's best

but i will look for you in this life and the next

— in this life and the next

<u>Day 86</u> March 28th, 08
sometime after lunch - how do I feel?
sad, worried, confused, crazy. I feel
buckin crazy, a little fucked up. My
appointment with ███████ was okay.
I talked to ███████ and I'm gonna have
to leave if I dont turn myself around
and ~~notice~~ take a step with fixing my
eating disorder. I feel so unmotivated
but fuck, I can do this. Even if I
have to fake it for a while. I need to
stay positive, and take care of myself.
No one can love me the way I need to
love myself. I feel like I've been at
the same spot for too long. I looked
when ███████ weighed me and it
was ███████ I got upset and I havnt
eaten much all day. I let this disorder
take over when I should be fighting
against it to be okay. I need help,

"You are officially the senior resident of the house," Jason said, beaming as he sat down opposite to me in a rickety green armchair.

The front room of the house was reserved for a few things.

There was a long brown couch that smelled slightly of mildew and cigarettes, a couple of tattered armchairs and an old metal elliptical machine that looked like something out of a 1950s gym.

We were allowed to come into this room on our personal time to read, write or try our luck at a workout from hell.

I had used the old machine, which was purely self-propelled, a couple of times. The sounds it would make upon its start made me wonder if it had a few extra screws dangling from the small black foot pads.

This room was also used for family visits or when someone was being sent home or when one of us would try to run away.

Runaways had only happened a few times since I had been here, but on all occasions, the kid would be brought back, usually by a couple of staff members and the police and be placed in this room until their parents or a family member could come collect them.

And although the rules were crystal clear about the boys and girls not touching each other, we had all heard stories of people sneaking in here and having sex.

It made the smell of the seat cushions a bit more unnerving at times.

A multi-purpose space, you could call it.

Today, Jason and I were meeting here for a therapy session.

Jason was one of the first counsellors I had met here, and even after our tense introduction regarding me being late to report downstairs, I had grown quite fond of him.

He had a mass of curly jet-black hair which he kept perfectly gelled on the top of his head.

We shared a mutual love of music and would often sit together while he played guitar and I frantically tried to come up with lyrics to his folky melodies.

He was alive and obnoxious in his enthusiasm while being able to turn his wit quickly into a firm and parental tone when needed.

And he was blunt.

I liked that about him.

I pushed my back into the lumpy cushion behind me, smiling at him, realizing he was right.

Now that Darcy had graduated, I was the senior here.

It was a big deal when one of us made it past the three-month mark.

"How are you feeling?" he asked, folding his hands together neatly and resting them in his lap.

"Good, I think," I said laughing slightly at the sound of my answer. I couldn't recall the last time I had been able to say that. It had been so hard for me to answer that question over the last few weeks. Knowing what I was feeling after spending so much time drowning myself in alcohol felt like quite the accomplishment in itself. I felt like a part of myself which had been kept frozen was slowly beginning to thaw.

"We need to talk about your weight."

His tone changed slightly, and I felt the mood of our conversation shift into some kind of seriousness.

He took a deep breath, clearly contemplating how to address me now, how to put into words what he obviously wanted to say.

What he had been waiting to say.

"The other staff and I have noticed a significant weight loss over the last few weeks. I'm concerned. We all are."

I looked away from him, shifting awkwardly in my seat on the couch as I tried to think of something to say.

Some kind of justification.

An excuse.

I had always been aware of how I looked, and tried — not that hard, really — to maintain some kind of figure.

A certain number.

But these last few weeks it wasn't really about a number anymore.

There is something that happens to you when you stop eating.

After the first few hours of initial hunger, fighting the urge to sneak into the kitchen at night or asking for one more helping of breakfast, there comes a certain stillness.

A euphoria, almost.

I had discovered recently that if I managed to get through an entire day, or even a couple of days, without consuming much, my mind would begin to quiet.

My body would begin to give up as its empty cries for fulfillment went unanswered.

My movements became slow but deliberate, and I felt as though the blood flowing through my veins was taking its time to reach its destination.

Everything was calm.

Everything became sort of okay.

For a little bit.

And when you don't feed yourself for a long period of time, it becomes harder to think about all of things that are wrong. All the things that went wrong. My mind would finally take rest from its seemingly constant state of panic. The only thing it seemed to be focused on was where the next meal was coming from.

How to get it or how to avoid it.

I became hyper-focused on the smallest and most minute details of each day in the hopes that I could schedule and manipulate each moment to suit what I needed to accomplish.

To stay empty.

They are going to force you to eat.

I looked to Jason, finally, wondering if I should tell him all of this, any of this.

"You've been doing amazing here," he said softly. "You've been working harder than anyone I've seen here in a while. I want you to succeed here, and when you leave here, but part of that is taking care of yourself…. If you're not eating, you're not going to be able to think."

That's the point.

I didn't know what to say.

I felt like a child getting caught for being sneaky.

And maybe that is kind of what it was.

He doesn't know what he's talking about; you're not that skinny.

I suddenly felt quite like that same child trying to hold onto something a parent was trying to take away. Something important. Something I needed.

Just tell him you'll eat… tell him you're sorry and that you'll try and then he'll stop asking you about it.

My inner voice felt calm and direct, however, I could sense a nervousness inside of me steadily rising to the surface.

How do I get away with this?

How do I hold onto the one thing that seemed to be getting me through being here?

It felt silly to think that my lack of eating was somehow becoming my saving grace, but it was more than that.

Much more than that.

After months of feeling like I was spinning out of control and slipping into the depths of complete and utter self-destruction, being physically empty was something I could grasp, something I could control.

It made me feel like I was in charge of my own life in some way.

I was the commander of my ship at last.

But how do you explain that to someone?

How do you make them understand that, without this, without this small piece of self-discipline, you're scared that you will fall apart?

Sitting in that room with Jason, I decided I wouldn't tell him how this felt inside of me.

I didn't think he would understand.

Or worse, he would understand and would spend the next month watching my every move.

Interrogating me at every meal.

So I lied.

"I'll try harder," I said quietly.

And in some ways, that was the truth.

I would try harder.

I would try harder to hold onto this part of myself that was finally beginning to settle.

I would try harder to hide the part of myself that was still silently screaming on the inside.

The walls of my chest seemed to constantly echo in bursts of rage and sadness, but when I was empty… everything just… went quiet.

And I needed that right now.

I desperately needed that.

Jason's eyes hovered over mine, surveying my expression and contemplating the words I had said. I wasn't sure if he believed me.

"If you don't work with us to make some changes here… you won't be able to stay."

He doesn't believe you.

No, they can't do that. I don't want to go back there, I thought frantically.

I need to stay here.

I'm not ready to go out there again.

And I need to finish the entire program. I still have things to work on, and I need to figure out where I'm going after this. I'm not ready.

My panic was obvious as I tried to catch my breath.

A hundred thoughts racing through my mind all at once.

"I don't want to leave," I said suddenly, my voice cracking.

His shoulders relaxed slightly. He took a deep breath in, releasing the obvious tension that had been building inside both of us.

"We're going to send you to see someone. A psychologist. She's in the next town over. The facility is going to cover the costs while you're here. Vikki will take you there next week for your first appointment."

I watched him watching me and wondered how this would help.

They think you're crazy.

"I'm not crazy," I said flatly, shifting my eyes away from his gaze.

"I know," he replied quietly, not wanting to put any kind of distance in our rapport. "Sometimes these things... these issues... can develop over time. I know you're not crazy."

His voice was warm and sincere as he leaned forward, trying to pull me into his words. To bring me back to some kind of understanding.

Some kind of compliance.

"Something happened to me a few months ago," I said slowly.

Don't do that.

Don't tell him.

I wasn't sure why I said that. I hadn't planned on telling him or anyone else here anything about that night.

I had been trying to push the memories far out of my mind, but they always just kind of hung there in the background.

No matter how much I tried to forget, I couldn't.

Some nights I would wake up and feel like I was still there, stumbling out of the café into the night.

I would shower in scalding hot water, trying to wash myself of the images. Burn his touch out of my skin.

Being here gave me so many things to focus on, and with each moment of our days planned down to the minute, I didn't always have to try very hard to distract myself.

But every day, in the quiet, early hours of the morning or the dark delivery of the night, she would speak to me.

Begging me to remember.

Cold.

Tiles.

Floor.

Blood.

No one believes you.

"I think I was raped."

The words spilled off of my tongue and caressed the air around us, dangling in the open room.

Finally.

I wasn't sure if I had ever said that word out loud before.

Jason eased back in his chair, taking a long slow breath, focusing his eyes on mine.

Maybe it all made sense to him now.

Maybe.

"There are certain things we, uh… aren't designed to help with…."

I could see him struggling with the words. "I think this is something you should talk about with the therapist… you know… explore a little more?"

Say nothing else.

I nodded to him, numb.

Awaiting the flow of tears that didn't come.

i wanted you to disappear
but it's not because i didn't want you here
i needed to hide you, sweet girl
i needed to keep you from this world
i closed the suitcase, boarded the door
shut all the windows, knelt on the floor
and i begged you to quiet your chatter
i pleaded with you to give up
don't tell them where you are going
or they will pull you back into the dark

— sick

"It's mail day!" Mallory shouted, as she twirled herself around the common room, brimming with excitement. Her dark brown hair bounced on her shoulders as she plopped herself down beside me on the old plaid couch.

This was one of the things we looked forward to the most here. Letters from the outside.

It was a bright and cheerful morning in the house.

The snow was beginning to melt outside on the country fields surrounding us, blades of grass reaching up to feel the sunlight after their long winter's sleep.

We had just finished our regular morning walk. The only time we were allowed to be that close to each other.

We walked in pairs, the long line of us, with staff members dispersed throughout and monitoring our movements and conversations but also taking in the vast newly-awakened greenery.

They often didn't notice when one of us would sway our arm casually against the person walking beside us.

It felt good to brush arms with someone.

A small amount of human connection.

There were only a few houses between the treatment centre and the two- or three-kilometre lane we would walk.

I wondered what the people who lived there thought of us.

A group of dishevelled teenagers being guided up and down a long dirt road.

This would have been a great opportunity for one of us to run away, but it didn't happen.

Not on our walks.

I think all of us were just happy to be outside and happy to be together.

Who would have thought?

We had all managed to find some kind of home amongst each other.

Bonding over our disrupted young lives and clinging to each other in almost every sense of the word.

The only time the counsellors would let us hug each other was if one of us was graduating.

Then and only then, after the ceremony had concluded, could we make our way over to the person who was leaving and embrace them.

I think that's why those moments meant so much more to us.

Not just because we could hold onto each other, but because we truly didn't know when we would see them again, if ever.

"You've got one!" Mallory said excitedly, pointing down the hallway towards the front of the house where the staff room was.

I must not have heard them call my name.

I got up and made my way down the hall to where Jason was standing and holding a small, perfectly square white envelope.

It didn't look like the letters I usually received.

My brother and sister and brother-in-law's family would write to me often.

I read and re-read their letters countless times.

It was one of the things that gave me the slightest bit of hope.

Hope in knowing that despite everything that had happened over the last few years, they were still there.

Sometimes my brother-in-law's mother would send me handwritten Bible verses. Pages upon pages of delicate cursive.

It must have taken her ages to write.

She would tell me about her life and how she had been brought to faith.

I wasn't a religious person in the devoted sense, but I loved that she would think of me and decide, even in the midst of her busy days and evenings, to sit down and write endless amounts of words to offer me some kind of peace, some kind of hope.

To this day, I have kept every letter she ever sent.

But this envelope in Jason's hands was different.

It was small, simple and thin, obviously lacking the pages of robust stories I was used to.

I was curious.

Jason turned the envelope over, showing a small, beautifully-written address of the treatment centre with no return address on the top corner. I recognized the handwriting immediately.

My father's.

It was not only customary, but a firm house rule, that we open all mail in front of a staff member.

I handed the envelope back to Jason, in typical fashion, as he carefully opened the neatly-packaged letter, holding it up to the light above us, scanning the front and back and finally opening the inside and shaking it meticulously.

I always wondered what he was looking for.

Maybe a gram of coke will magically fall out of the page.

Well, stranger things have happened.

Jason brought the letter back down, obviously satisfied with his inspection, and handed it back to me.

The front of the card had a bright yellow sunflower photographed with a brilliant blue sky cascading above it.

I opened the card and on the inside were just four words, delicately written in the centre of the card:

I believe in you

I sat there for a long time looking over the words in front of me.

The simple way his handwriting glided along the page.

I pictured him picking out this card.

A sunflower.

That that in itself could still remind him of me was both magnificent and heartbreaking all at once.

I pictured him sitting at his desk, thinking of what to write.

What do you say to your estranged daughter who you hadn't seen in months?

I'm sure he thought about it for a while.

He was always thinking.

Whatever he had been thinking about that day, something inside of him must have thought that through everything we had been through, I should surely be reminded that he believed I could keep going.

That I could get through this.

And the next thing that life would push towards me.

And I thought about my parents.

I thought being six years old and my father setting up our living room to resemble some kind of movie theatre.

We couldn't afford to go out to a cinema, so he made little tickets and big bowls of popcorn and put a gate up in the doorway that led from the kitchen into our little living room.

He and my mother had each of us line up, jumping with excitement as he opened the gate. One by one, the three of us filed into the living room, giving him a ticket and then pretending to buy popcorn. We would all take our places on our lumpy grey couch, bouncing happily in our seats and awaiting the movie to start playing on our old and desperately small television.

I thought about the time when he found out that someone had stolen money from me at school.

I left out the part where I had given this person the money to buy alcohol and they never returned with it.

This was before I had discovered the brilliance of a fake ID.

He asked for the person's name and spent weeks contacting their parents, even their boyfriend, in an attempt to get it back.

One afternoon, I had come home from school to find an envelope in the mailbox that was addressed to me.

As I opened it I saw the money I had been missing.

Fifty dollars.

This was a lot when you were fifteen.

It would be quite a few years before my father would admit to me that he had placed the envelope in our mailbox and used his money.

He hadn't wanted me to carry the burden of a burnt bridge.

I looked up from the card, my eyes beginning to burn with fresh tears that were making their journey up from my heart.

They are still there.

She was talking about my parents.

And they were still there, weren't they?

Even though the chaos that had divided us felt entirely insurmountable at times, I wondered if they were just people after all.

When you strip away the labels and the expectations, however warranted in their roles, I wondered what my father had been through in this life that caused him to relentlessly try to drown away his pain.

And I thought of what my mother had had to overcome in her life and how difficult it was for them to relate to me.

And maybe the difficulty didn't really lay in their ability to understand, but in their desperate desire to keep their children away from anything that would lead them off the carefully laid path they had set out for us.

To do well in school, to become as educated as you could, to get a good job, to find a partner that was strong, steady and stable who would withstand the storms of life.

I think that's what every parent wants for their child.

Especially if they didn't have that themselves or had to struggle to receive it.

And I guess each new generation of parents is plagued with the same task.

To try as hard as they can to reduce the burden placed onto their children's shoulders.

To teach them how to become.

I knew in that moment that their intentions were good.

Even if the message became tangled and frayed in the details of a life being lived.

Call them.

Maybe I should.

At least to tell them that I was okay.

i have always been scared to find you
to see you looking back at me
if i could count the times i'd felt safe with you
more than 1
and less than 3
and while my mind will tell me
that i have to go
that i must leave every space
i wonder if one of these fall afternoons
you will come find me
here in my place

— less than 3

I opened the door to my room, stepped inside and heaved my bag from my shoulders, letting it thud heavily on the floor.

My little apartment on the top floor of the shelter.

It only took about ten steps to walk from one end to the other, but it was complete with a bed, a desk, a little kitchen and a bathroom.

A few of us lived up here, the older ones.

The rest of the younger girls lived downstairs in the shared rooms.

It was easier to keep an eye on them that way.

Of the few of us who lived upstairs, I spoke to no one.

I barely talked to the staff, who were here twenty-four hours day monitoring the comings and goings of each of us.

I had been sober for nine months and wanted to keep it that way.

Though the other girls here seemed nice enough, I would sometimes hear them in the courtyard below, just outside my window, talking loudly about the boys they liked or the places they were going during the day while secretly drinking vodka coolers from plastic water bottles.

A part of me wanted to get to know them.

It was lonely here sometimes, and although I tried my best to busy myself with meetings and schoolwork, in the evenings when I would come home to the quiet little eight by twelve space that was now my home, I wanted to be able to call on one of those girls and just sit and talk.

To have someone to chain-smoke cigarettes with, hanging our heads out of our room windows, telling stories about how we got here and sharing secrets.

I missed Ray for that.

I hadn't heard from her while I was in the treatment centre, and although I missed her terribly, I thought now maybe the distance was for the best.

I was scared that if we were together again, I would want to drink, and I knew she would support me in whatever I wanted to do whether that was being sober or being drunk.

And I didn't feel strong enough to stand up for myself if I were in a situation like that.

The shelter sat on a quiet little street in the heart of the city. I would sometimes forget I was so deep in the downtown core because of how quiet and peaceful it was upstairs in my little apartment.

When I came home in the afternoons I would often sit and write, and when I was done with that I would walk, sometimes for hours, exploring the incredible, bustling city.

One of the shelter staff had given me a piece of paper with a long list of all the different soup kitchens in the downtown area. At first, I had shrugged it off, stuffing the piece of paper into my bag on my way out, but after about a week of being here I was glad I had kept it.

I had managed to keep my old job at the grocery store for the first couple of months after leaving treatment, but as the weeks went on and my weight continued to decline, Nina and I both agreed I should focus on graduating from school first.

I had never been on welfare before.

Nina and I had gone through the application process together and had it set up so that each month three hundred dollars would be sent directly to the shelter, as required, and the remaining $247 was mine to pay for food, a cell phone and anything else I might need throughout the month.

I didn't have much experience with budgeting or paying bills, and I am no mathematician, but living on $247 a month didn't sound possible.

But I did.

For quite a while.

The piece of paper with the list of soup kitchens proved to be very handy around this time.

I quickly started to get to know the best ones to go to.

The small, narrow church on the corner of one of the busiest intersections was great because there were computers with working internet, and if I got there just after lunchtime, there would be hardly anyone there.

The food was bland — massive pots of soup that never seemed to be quite hot enough and bread that had been donated from a local bakery hours away from being too stale to bite into.

One of the bigger churches in Chinatown offered an all-day drop-in and served two meals a day, breakfast and lunch, and their food was worth the five-kilometre hike from the shelter.

One of the ladies there would let me take a few extra slices of bread with me when I was leaving.

I often declined, but she was so adamant and I could tell it made her feel good when I accepted, even hesitantly.

"You'll starve out there, Sweetie, take it," she would say quietly, not wanting to draw attention to herself.

I tried my best to keep to myself during my travels, only speaking when spoken to and avoiding eye contact with the older people who had clearly seen their fair share of troubles in life and probably weren't used to this little eighteen-year-old sharing their space with them.

My clothes dangled from my wasted frame, and although I told myself I looked amazing, I can see now that the stares I received were more out of concern than attraction.

My favourite part of the day was about 7:00 p.m. when I could start getting myself ready to go to a meeting.

Vikki and Jason had both told me I needed to go to meetings once I left treatment. Well, they didn't say it like that.

What they said was, "You'll probably die if you don't have a support network, so go to meetings. Every single day, twice a day if you need to."

And it wasn't that I didn't have support.

I knew my sister and brother-in-law were hurt that I didn't want to continue living with them.

I thought I could do it and tried after leaving treatment.

I remember the night I left the centre, the car pulling off the old gravel driveway, slowly making its way towards the highway.

It had taken about forty minutes from leaving the facility to approach that familiar suburban landscape, and in the darkness that laced overtop of it, I had foolishly convinced myself that I could do this.

I could stay there.

I could start over.

Hours later, as the sunshine swept its way into the apartment living room and I stepped outside to greet it, everything was illuminated once more.

The memories.

The memory.

I knew then how stupid I had been for thinking I could stay there.

So close to where my life had fallen apart.

You won't make it.

She was right. I wouldn't.

I needed to go somewhere else, away from there.

At least for a while.

I hoped that one day I would be able to sit down with my sister and explain everything.

Tell her why I couldn't be in that part of the city anymore.

About how something so simple like taking a bus or walking down one of the streets close to my old school or close to where it happened would send me into a state of panic.

Constantly looking over my shoulder, reminding myself to breathe, pressing my fingernails into the palms of my hands and trying to control my tears.

And maybe that's what I should have done.

But I was trying my hardest to forget something terrible, and the very last thing I thought I should do was talk about it.

To give it life.

It had already lived lifetimes inside of me.

Every muscle, every bone in my body, remembered that night.

So it was quite the task convincing my mind that it never happened.

And I almost managed to do it.

Almost.

Date: Sept 22nd/08

I feel like I should introduce myself all over again, but I just couldn't stand the thought of going through the story from the start, so lets start today. I haven't journalled in so long. Random things have been coming out in poems and messed up conversations.

I'm not sure where to begin. Its a freedom to know that I could just get up from my bed and walk all over the city. I can do whatever I want. I'm kind of sad that ████ didn't call me today but all in all - its been a good day. A little anxious cuz I ate a bit today but thats okay. I'm doing a bunch of walking tomorrow so that'll make up for it.

one day you will look down from your tower and see
all of the battles you once faced
all of the dragons you once slayed
and scattered at its base
are the footprints of those still there
wandering through the alleys
abandoned in the streets
i hope that when that day comes
you will remember where you once stood
and drop the ladder

— ladders

Date: Dec. 2nd, 08

Today has been interesting. I went to the hospital and talked. I left early. I dont know, I just dont even want to talk about it. ███████ called me last night, just crying because of my weight. I wanted to scream. when people really put themselves out there in front of me, I find it really difficult. Anyways, I'm in Timmies waiting for ███████ Its ███████ and ███████ celebration tonight! Toronto called me and said I could come early. I was so scared I said no but I'll talk to ███████ I wanna wait till January. Anyways, tomorrow I finally get to meet with my ow worker! @ 9:30am and then I'm gonna go to school and work on King Lear. I dont have much time to finish it but I'll pray for the motivation and courage to do it. ███████ called me and, hes coming to the meeting

I stood up from my chair, along with everyone else, as the meeting came to a close.

I was new to this group, and it took about half an hour on the bus to get here from the shelter, but I liked it.

I had started coming every week, every Tuesday.

I had spent the last few months travelling around to different meetings trying to figure out which ones I liked.

Which ones felt welcoming and safe.

Before I left the centre, Vikki had told me to go to meetings where people had been sober for a long time and to try to find women who had something I wanted.

I think what she meant was find someone who was honest.

Someone who was relatively happy.

Someone who spoke about gratitude and tried to remain positive even through the storms.

Find other people who were living the way I wanted to live.

People who took care of themselves and their families.

People who took the cards they were dealt with grace and patience and who truly lived in such a way that it made those around them want to do better as well.

And I did find those people.

Both inside and outside of those meetings.

And in the years to come they would raise me into a strong and resilient women. Into someone who could pay bills on time, someone who my friends and family could rely on.

Someone who discovered how to tell the truth.

Someone who learned how to care for myself and those around me.

But on this cool fall evening, I was eighteen years old and still hadn't quite figured out how to eat a meal without throwing it up.

"Hey! You're new here?"

I turned around to see a man standing behind me, his hand outstretched in welcome.

"Sort of," I said, casually extending my hand into his.

"Do you happen to have an extra cigarette?" he asked.

"Oh… yeah, one sec," I said reaching into my bag and pulling out a tattered pack.

I opened it and handed one to him.

He smiled, taking it and opening his mouth to speak again when suddenly another man appeared beside him, placing a large, firm hand on my shoulder.

He was much older than both of us and wore a long, dark blue wool coat with a scarf that had been carefully wrapped around his neck with each side of it perfectly positioned along the coat lapels.

"Nice to see you again," he said loudly, his voice booming over the chatter around us.

I had never seen this man before.

But something about this encounter made me feel as if he knew something I didn't.

I smiled at him, quickly glancing down at his shoes, which were polished to perfection.

The ceiling lights above us dancing in their reflection.

The other man with the cigarette backed away slowly, nodding to the two of us nervously before making his way towards the exit.

That was weird.

"My name is Brian," the man said warmly, surveying my appearance.

I adjusted my jacket slightly and pulled my bright purple hair around the base of my neck, nervously trying to occupy my hands.

"Why do you think, out of all the people here, that man chose to come ask you for a cigarette?"

"Oh… I'm not sure…," I said nervously, scanning the others around us.

There were quite a lot of people here.

Maybe he had seen me smoking outside before the meeting and figured I had some extras.

Brian peered down at me from his thick-rimmed glasses before continuing.

"There are at least twenty other men here who all smoke," he said, lowering his voice slightly and leaning closer to me. "But he came to ask you because you're young and you're pretty."

"Oh…," I said, suddenly feeling stupid.

"Not everyone here has good intentions. So next time an older man seeks you out in a meeting and asks for a cigarette, say no," he said firmly, "and tell him to fuck off if you want," he added, lowering his voice again slightly and revealing just a bit of a smirk.

I was surprised by his use of profanity.

For some reason I hadn't expected a man dressed as he was to be using that kind of language. My parents always used to say it made you sound uneducated.

I spotted a thick, heavy looking watch on his right wrist.

He did not look uneducated.

"How long have you been coming here?" he asked.

"A few months," I said, straightening my shoulders. "How...
how long have you been coming here?" I asked, realizing that
we were both, in fact, at an AA meeting.

"Oh, a few years," he smiled.

I wondered what brought him here.

I guess the same reason any of us ended up in meetings like this
at different points in our lives.

Some kind of trauma and chaos that left us a little broken, and
for some reason, the dingy church basement was one of the last
possible places that could help us.

"So, what are you going to do now?"

I didn't quite understand what he meant by that.

The way he asked the question made me wonder if he was
talking about tonight or in general.

Either way, it was a difficult question to answer.

He must have noticed my obvious confusion, as he smiled
broadly and asked again, this time more specifically, "Well, now
that you're moving on with your life. What are you going to do
with it?"

That was certainly a very big question.

What was I going to do?

I thought about that all the time now but couldn't seem to land
on an answer, on some kind of clear path.

I knew I would need to finish high school, get a job, move out
of the shelter.... Eventually.

"I'm not sure," I said quietly, holding his gaze. "I want to figure
some things out, I guess.... Where I'll live, getting a job." I
sounded off the two first things that came to mind.

"Then I guess you better start planting some seeds, kid," he said
warmly, before tapping my shoulder gingerly and offering one

last big smile before he turned slightly away and greeted another group of people who were passing us on their way towards the exit.

Plant some seeds?

It took me a long time to figure out what he meant by that.

2:34 am

Date: DeC. 27th, 08

    I really should be sleeping. I plan on it soon because tomorrow morning I'm going out for ~~a~~ breakfast and ~~a~~ meeting with ████. I'm happy, it should be great! Well tonight Mary and I went out for coffee and she wasn't feeling good so we sat and talked for a while. It was really nice. I went to a meeting with ████ the one at St. Basil's, and holy crap was it ever good. I got a copy of the 12 & 12, so I'm going to ~~steert~~ reading step one daily, and doing inventories. I worked out for a while cuz I was feeling F*T. I feel better now. A little sad, cuz I can see how Dad is suffering, but its times like these I need to be strong. This cute guy added me on facebook so that was nice. ████ sent me a message saying he loved my writing. Sometimes, despite all these good things, I just want to die. I don't know where that comes from.

I pulled the heavy metal door open and was met with a sudden burst of warmth as I quickly pushed myself into the lobby and away from the freezing winter street.

It must have been -25°C today, and the walk from the shelter to the welfare office was worse than I remembered.

I hadn't been here in a few weeks.

My worker had given me time from trying to find a job so I could try to finish my high school classes, which was proving to be more difficult than I had thought.

But it saved me from having to report into her every month.

Today I had made my way down to the office to talk to my worker about getting a regular bus pass, but the bus drivers had gone on strike recently, halting all regular service around the city.

No one seemed to know when the strike would end, but for now, it meant there wasn't much use trying to get a bus pass.

I wanted to come to the meeting anyway.

I liked talking to Gwen.

She always seemed interested in how I was doing and how things were going at the shelter.

I would see other people come and go quickly from their meetings with their workers, but Gwen never seemed to be in a rush.

I liked that about her.

I made my way up the staircase to the second floor and through another set of doors that led into the main waiting area.

I carefully surveyed the room, wondering if I would see anyone I knew from the soup kitchens.

I usually ran into a few of them down here.

As I made my way over to the front desk to sign in, I noticed a girl who was not much older than me make her way from the sign-in desk as she moved past me to find a seat amongst the rows of others.

She didn't look at me, but as she passed by, a soft, sweet and almost summery smell swept its way from her.

Perfume.

It was beautiful.

She was wearing a gorgeous long black coat.

I recognized the brand.

I had always wanted a coat like that but they were almost four hundred dollars.

I used to tell myself that one day when I had a job and some extra money, I would save for a coat like that. One to feel pretty in.

I adjusted my bag awkwardly on my shoulder as I approached the sign-in desk, waiting for the receptionist to acknowledge me.

She had her back turned to me and was whispering with a co-worker, giggling and scoffing at the same time.

I leaned in slightly to try and hear what they were talking about.

"You say you don't have any money but you're over here with a jacket like that? C'mon."

The girl with her back to me was nodding her head in agreement as she slowly turned to face me. She had a look on her face that I had seen so many times recently.

One I didn't think we were supposed to see here.

Judgement.

I must have had some kind of look of confusion on my face as the receptionist pulled her chair closer to the desk, closer to me, before meeting my gaze and saying, "Some people, eh?"

But she wasn't talking about her friend.

Her friend who made the shitty comment.

She was talking about the girl with the nice jacket.

Bitch.

I turned my head to look back towards the girl with the coat, who was now sitting a few rows away from us.

I hoped she hadn't heard what they had said.

I don't think she did.

I turned back towards the receptionist and handed her my ID card, giving an awkward smile and trying to be polite without making it seem like I agreed with her.

I didn't want to fight with the staff who stood between me and buying my ten apples for the month. Between me and getting a bus pass for the buses that don't run. Between me and being able to stay at the shelter.

It's not good to start fights with those people.

We all knew that.

Everyone in rows one to five.

But up here, at the reception desk, I wondered if this was what they all thought of us.

You're not allowed to have nice things if you're poor.

I guess not.

I didn't wonder how that girl had gotten her nice coat.

It was probably the same way I had gotten my nice boots.

Someone close to me, Grace, had bought them for me one day when she saw my tattered shoes covered in snow.

And maybe no one bought it for her, maybe she bought it herself after working a cash job.

Maybe someone gave her money for her birthday.

Maybe why does it fuckin matter?

It doesn't.

I didn't think about how that girl got her coat, but I did think about she felt in her coat.

I imagined her putting it on in her little apartment.

And her apartment would probably be in a neighbourhood that wasn't very nice, like most of our apartments.

Maybe it wasn't even an apartment. That was, after all, a luxury for most of us.

Maybe it was a small, simple room.

The sounds, smells and images around her might be stressful and fill her with anxiety.

But maybe when she puts on that coat she feels confident just for a moment. Powerful.

And it keeps her warm and it makes her feel pretty and I think that's a good thing.

Maybe it makes her happy.

But you can't be that happy when you're poor.... Not in front of them.

And I wondered how I hadn't seen it before.

The divide between us and them.

"She's ready for you."

I glanced to the receptionist, who was pointing across the desk to her right. Gwen was standing in the reception area, smiling, waving me over.

I made my way over to Gwen, returning her warm smile as we walked together down the hallway towards her cubicle.

"It's cold out today, isn't it?"

She always started our meetings talking about the weather.

"It's a bad one today," I smiled. We turned a corner at the end of the hall and made our way into her cubicle area.

She had a window office, which always made me feel more comfortable.

I'd had other workers who were sandwiched right in the middle of this place, and it always felt a bit claustrophobic.

"So, let's talk about how things are going at the shelter."

Gwen began moving a few stacks of paperwork to her desk, placing them neatly between us, and she turned to find a pen. There was always something to sign.

"It's good…. Quiet…. I'm trying to finish my English course right now, but I can't get to school so they gave me the books to take home."

"Oh, well that is great news!" Gwen beamed. "And are you still going to the meetings?" she asked, looking over to me as she leaned back into her chair.

"Yeah, every day… sometimes twice a day," I laughed, thinking about all the walking I had been doing.

"That's good…. Are they helping?"

Yes.

"Yeah…."

And that was the truth.

They had been helping.

But mostly in ways I wasn't even sure I needed.

Sometimes I felt like a fraud going there.

I was this little, inexperienced, eighteen-year-old "alcoholic,"

yet somehow when I spoke to people there about some

of the things I had done, or the things they had done, an overwhelming sense of peace came over me.

I didn't have to try to be anything or anyone else.

I didn't have to explain myself.

And I could have friends.

I could make real friends.

It was giving me that.

I didn't realize how incredibly lonely I had been until I started spending more time with people in those meetings.

Sometimes it's easier to keep it together in the treatment centres.

And maybe those meetings wouldn't be the place where I would find my comfort forever, but for now…. For now… those meetings were the only place that I felt safe.

"I'm almost a year sober…," I said suddenly, realizing how close we were to my new birthday.

"Oh, that's so fantastic!" Gwen's eyes lit up as she patted my hands which rested on the table between us.

I didn't think she was allowed to do that, but I didn't mind.

It felt so nice to have a worker who treated me like a regular person.

"Now, I did want to talk to you about something else today while we're here," she said. Her tone was different than what I was used to, quieter almost. "I know the last time you were here you had talked about meeting with a doctor to address your eating disorder."

I was suddenly very uncomfortable.

I remembered having this conversation with Gwen a while ago.

Something inside of me that day had thought it was okay to be vulnerable about this.

To tell someone the one thing I didn't want to discuss in any kind of detail.

Anytime I opened my mouth to anyone about the eating, I would regret it immediately.

It felt like I needed to hide her.

I needed to protect her.

That part of me that was trying to live while trying to die all at the same time.

And if I talk to you about it, you'll try to take it away from me.

You'll tell me I'm sick and that I need help, but you'll never ask me how it feels inside of me.

You won't ask me how much it has helped.

Because that sounds crazy, doesn't it?

And I didn't know how to put any of this into words that made sense.

Maybe in those brief moments when I would admit that something was wrong… maybe then I could see it for what it was… just for a moment… maybe then I wanted help.

But those moments would come and they would go and I would cling to my excuses once again.

Don't tell her that they called you.

"I haven't met with them yet…. I'm… I'm not sure if I can right now…,"

They're going to try and send you to the hospital.

They can't do that, I thought to myself.

Maybe not yet, but they could try.

Maybe they'll cut your cheque if you're not following the rules.

Make something up.

About not going to the doctor yet.

"I think that would be a lot to deal with right now on top of still being new in recovery," I said, sounding confident. I knew from the look on her face that Gwen believed the lie immediately.

"Do you feel like your recovery is at risk?"

"I mean, I dunno… right now is kind of hard… the bus strike makes it difficult to get to the usual meetings I had gone to before… I can't do a lot of school right now either... I just feel a bit stuck... kind of depressed maybe."

"Do you think some kind of relapse prevention program might help?"

Say yes… it's better than the hospital.

"Maybe we can get you into a place that can focus on the eating as well as the addiction?"

Call the place you went to last year… when you were seventeen. You'll be able to workout there and they don't watch what you eat.

That's fucked up, I thought back to myself.

I should be trying to find a spot that has different kinds of treatment, like she said.

It's either this or they send you to the fuckin hospital in a few months.

They're not gonna send me to a hospital, calm down. They don't have the authority to do that.

Play that game if you want to… but if they think you're healthy and refusing treatment, they'll put you on someone else's caseload who will make you look for work.

I have to finish school first.

You think they care about that?

Your cheque will get cut off every month if you're not doing what they say when they say it.

She had a point.

Gwen was considered a "specialized" worker who didn't have to follow the same rules as the others. She worked with people who were having addiction problems. If I said I was doing fine, she would have to transfer me to a regular worker.

Don't kid yourself, you're a number here.

And what else do you have going on?

Nothing.

The buses aren't running, you can't do school, you have no excuses left not to go see the doctors.

You think little Gweny over here is gonna keep being this nice to you all the time if you keep saying no?

They call it non-compliance.

K, relax, I'll figure it out.

No, WE are figuring it out.

"I'm gonna make some phone calls tonight and see if I can find a place with a bed open," I said, leaning back in my chair and hoping my inner voice would quiet.

Maybe it wouldn't be so bad going away again.

It would buy me some time.

The centre in the next city was only a few weeks long, and I knew if I called, they would probably take me pretty quickly.

And maybe I could go there and just take a break and figure out how I'm going to talk to the doctor at the hospital and what I need to do to fix the eating issues.

Whether I liked it or not, I couldn't keep going like this.

"Well, you just let me know what you hear, and we can certainly help with the Greyhound fare."

Will do.

<u>Jan 14th, 2009</u>
Good morning sunshine! It's
the first class of the day. I finished writing my letter, and now we
have group therapy I believe. I started praying that I would be able to
breathe, and guess what? I can!
It was so strange, I have to tell
████ I pushed my lip ring back
in and I kinda like it. It hurt a
little bit but thats okay. I had a
nice conversation with ████████
in the cab
We had lunch and we're in women and
Relationships. We did that sticky note
thing where we put our names in a hat
and get sticky notes to stick positive
comments on people. I'll show you
later. :)

Do you really think it's a problem?

… the eating?

I'm not sure.

I mean, yeah, I guess it is.

It must be.

Says who?

Says everyone!

This isn't normal, right?

You're not even that small.

People are overreacting and you fuckin know it.

What if they're not though?

What if they see something that I… can't see?

Yeah okay, cuz you can't look in a mirror, she laughed.

You and I see what the truth is, so don't go making this into something it's not.

I worked out for three hours today.

And you'll do it again tomorrow.

Stop being such a fuckin baby.

God, you're the worst.

Always complaining about everything.

I'm hungry.

And you haven't worked hard enough to deserve the fuckin cracker that came with your soup at dinner tonight.

This was supposed to be a good thing… coming here.

And it is.

You did the right thing.

But you can't tell anyone about the eating… or the binging… or the exercising.

Then what was the point?

You said you wanted a break, right?

This is your break.

Stay here for a while, away from everyone back home.

You know eventually you'll have to be admitted.

Don't let them take me away from you yet.

I won't.

Are you sure?

You came pretty fuckin close to talking about it in group again yesterday.

Everything hurts.

Everything hurt before.

I'll help you through this.

We'll get to the other side together.

And when is that gonna be?

Getting to the other side?

But she couldn't tell me that.

She could never fuckin tell me when it would end.

I printed off the chords for Now &
Then, and it looks pretty easy. On
another subject, we're talking about
abuse, and I don't know why I just
can't connect to what happened in
07. I hear people talking about it,
and I think about it sometimes but
I just can't cry. I mean it's been
a little while, and I'm just waiting
for something to happen so I can have
a good cry. I'm glad it's wednes-
day though. When we get back to
to the house - after dinners theres
the 3 headed dragon movie, so
when I get back I'll work out
for a bit, and re-read parts of
Twilight, organize my things, etc.

i wanted you to fix me
i wrote it in big bold letters
satin red lipstick
all over the walls
maybe i can be better
maybe i can be something
if you'd just stay beside me
i'd be anything you want
and we mould each other gently
push each other fiercely
angry with the replicas we've made
because i've told you my story
but you still just don't know me
and i wasn't listening anyways

— 333

Seven months later.

and just like that you were gone
and as the memory fades
and i sink back into the ground
the hole becoming deeper
the scar becoming brighter
i wonder if we ever knew each other
i wonder if through all of our time
was i just looking for myself
when what i found was someone else?

—you

"You've been advised that you've had a major depressive episode?" the doctor said plainly, not moving her gaze from a stack of paperwork in her hands. I couldn't tell whether this was a question or a statement.

What the fuck is a depressive episode?

Like you get it for thirty minutes and then it goes away?

I remembered sitting in front of a computer in a doctor's office waiting area in one of the treatment centres, filling out a questionnaire.

It took almost a full hour of rotating through question after question which asked about how sad I had felt that week or that month.

I remembered a slightly ancient looking male doctor going over the results with me in an appointment that lasted less than five minutes and announcing that I must be clinically depressed.

I never saw that doctor again.

This doctor, a woman whose office I had been to only once before, seemed to have gotten a copy of that consultation.

If you could call it that.

I had met with her when I was seventeen while I was in the other treatment centre.

The appointment Jason and Vikki had arranged so I could talk to someone about my eating issues.

She had a second office located in the city, a few bus rides away from my apartment.

The one with the heavy blue door.

The one Dillon and I moved into.

I still couldn't believe he was gone.

"Have you considered trying medication?" she said casually, glancing up at me momentarily from behind the documents.

Yeah, maybe if you have one that can knock me out.

"No," I said firmly. "I don't think that's what I need right now. I just want to get through school and start looking for a job maybe later this year."

"Well," she sighed, pushing her glasses from her eyes and resting them on the top of her head, "I think we have a lot of work to do before that can happen. The history with your family, you're still relatively new in sobriety, and it looks as if you've been losing more weight since I last saw you."

I sat, silently, breaking her gaze as I shifted uncomfortably in my chair.

She was right.

You're not that new in sobriety.

It's been over two years now.

But she's right about the weight, I thought.

I hadn't been eating at all during the day, and when I did finally break the cycle some evenings, I would eat more food than was reasonable for any sized person. Followed immediately by an hour of forcing myself to throw up and following that with a two- or three-hour walk.

I was constantly exhausted.

My hair was beginning to fall out in long and disturbing clumps.

My hands would shake the moment I woke up, and the tips of my fingers were somehow always cold.

And as you read this you might ask yourself, *Well, why didn't she just eat?*

Why didn't she just eat a small amount at a time and not be so concerned with her looks?

But the thing is, the thing I was beginning to understand, was that it was never about that.

It was never about the food.

It was never about how I looked.

Maybe on the surface.

Maybe as something tangible my mind could hold onto to somehow justify the way I was living.

Something I could look in the mirror and see and know that what I was doing was somehow working.

But I know that it wasn't about the way I looked because I couldn't see myself anymore.

The comments I would receive about needing to "eat a burger" or "see a doctor" did not affect me the way the statement giver intended.

It only made me feel as if I was winning.

And winning at what?

Winning at disappearing.

If you tell me I look awful, if you tell me I look sick, then you are acknowledging to me that you see the same pain that I feel.

Finally.

Finally, someone can see it.

And while this momentary validation was stunning, it made my heart ache all the same because I could no longer see myself.

I could no longer see my own pain.

I was still pretending that it didn't exist.

"I think we need to talk about having you referred to the hospital eating disorders program."

No.

We're not going away again.

No more centres.

No more rehab.

No more.

"What program is that?" I asked hesitantly.

"There are two. One is where you attend the hospital during the day and then return home at night. The other is where you live at the hospital for a period of time."

Absolutely fuckin not.

What are they going to do there?

Force feed you?

"No, I really don't think I'm ready for that right now," I said quietly.

There was a long pause, and I desperately wanted to fill it with something.

Some kind of comment or stupid joke.

That was usually how I handled uncomfortable silences, but today I had nothing to say.

I had come into this appointment feeling hopeful that she would have some kind of motivational message for me.

That's what brain doctors are for, right?

But I didn't want to hear the message she was delivering today.

And I didn't want to have this conversation.

The one where she tries to make me healthy by attempting to rid me of the one thing that felt like it was helping.

And in that moment, I wondered if I had simply traded one vice for another.

Had I really just spent all this time trading a drinking problem for an eating disorder?

"Okay," she said finally, putting her clipboard and the stack of paperwork beside her on a small wooden desk. "How have you been feeling this week?"

I feel nothing.

I feel nothing.

i made a deal with you that night
placing my left hand over your heart
hope to die
and all the rest
i would give you every one of my tomorrows
if you just save me from today
and you laughed
and you laughed
lifting my chin to see your face
but it was a mirror there in its place

— *396*

He placed the big black bag down on the floor beside my bed.

It looked more like an accordion or some kind of old-fashioned suitcase.

I wondered what he kept in there.

I thought better than to ask that right now.

It was our first meeting, after all.

"You're eighteen?" he asked, looking up from his cell phone.

You already told him your age.

"Nineteen," I corrected firmly, straightening my back and relaxing my shoulders.

He was much taller than I was, and I was suddenly feeling rather small in his presence.

He stared at me for what felt like too long before moving towards me and bending down to pick up the big black suitcase.

He walked over to my dresser, which was the only clear surface in the apartment.

I didn't have a coffee table.

I think you need a real living room for one of those.

I watched him carefully lift the black bag up, placing it on top of the old wooden dresser.

The one that had been painted over white far too many times.

The way he was handling this bag made it seem like something awfully delicate was inside.

There was a zipper on the top of the bag, right by the handle.

I watched him slowly tilt the bag onto its side before pulling the zipper all the way around and pushing the top of the bag open.

I stayed standing behind him but pushed myself up to my tiptoes to see what was inside.

A camera.

A very expensive looking camera with some kind of giant lightbulb attached to this other umbrella looking thing.

Didn't think he was actually a professional.

He began taking the pieces out of the bag, one by one, assembling.

I could feel my heartbeat starting to quicken, suddenly remembering what we had agreed to.

What he was here for.

Calm down.

It's just photos.

Right, I thought.

Just pictures.

I can do this.

You have to do this.

Maybe I could wait a bit… tell him I'm not feeling well or something.

I could feel my body starting to vibrate.

It always started in my chest and then seemed to radiate out, all the way to my toes.

It made my feet feel like they were being pushed down to the ground while the rest of my body floated away from me.

Or maybe it was just my mind floating away from my body.

I had learned how to do that.

Make my mind just float away for a while.

But whenever I felt that heavy, anxious feeling in my chest, I always wondered if I should try to run.

You can't back out now, idiot, he's already here.

She was right.

It would be awkward now to ask him to leave.

We had planned this over a week ago, and he really did seem eager to get here.

Just breathe.

You need the money.

Money isn't fuckin everything, is it? I thought back to myself.

It is when you don't have any.

Don't forget that roll of toilet paper in your bathroom you stole from a church yesterday.

Fuck.

I thought about what was left in my bank account.

I had paid the rent yesterday. That was five hundred.... That left forty-seven dollars for the rest of the month... I could go to the soup kitchen for lunch for the rest of the week... I could sell a few things... maybe I could find a house to clean next week and make some cash.

Your phone bill is due tomorrow and the electricity in a week.

Who the fuck are you going to call about a job with no phone?

Do this now... maybe a couple times and just get ahead until we can figure something else out.

"Are you ready?"

I looked up at him, removing myself from my inner conversation.

The one that never seemed to end.

I looked down at his hands, seeing them holding that pristine looking camera that was now fully assembled with the big light.

I was pretty sure I had told him I had done this before.

I didn't want to come off as inexperienced and young. That's how you get robbed.

I nodded to him, walking over to my bed.

I assumed this is where he would want me to be.

I stood at the edge of that simple black futon for a moment, wondering how I would do this.

How I would be able to keep the anxiety at bay.

The feelings, the thoughts, my mind, I needed it all to be calm right now.

Just for a while.

Just for an hour.

Just enough time for us to get through this.

As I stood with my back to Pablo, I thought about what someone else would do. Someone who had done this before. And really done it, not just lied about it.

Just breathe.

I followed her instructions and took a deep breath in, and as I exhaled, I heard the click of the camera behind me.

It's starting.

I grazed my hands along the bottom of my shirt and slowly started to lift it up, up and over my head, letting it slip from my hands and fall to the ground.

I reached an arm around behind me and felt for the clasp of my bra.

I started to undo it, slowly, as the clicks of the camera increased.

As I undid the clasp and felt the bra slide from my body and fall away, I noticed something was missing.

My mind.

She was quiet.

Silent.

It happened…. She floated away.

I spent the rest of that hour without her.

Without myself.

And I missed her in some odd way, but she was too loud to be with me in times like these.

I knew that.

I leaned myself onto the bed, turning myself around as the clicking continued. Pablo was focused, deliberate in his work as he moved closer to me.

And even as he crouched behind the expensive camera, capturing this moment with me, I could tell he couldn't see me. When you disconnect from yourself so casually, it almost feels comforting to see someone do the same.

When it was over, he handed me two hundred dollars. Enough to pay my cell phone bill and the electricity, and I could even buy a really good pack of cigarettes.

I pushed myself up in the bed, glancing over to Pablo as he began the tedious process of dismantling the camera.

"I'll see you next week," he said casually, looking over to me.

I couldn't read him at all.

No hint of thought or depth behind his eyes.

I didn't remember agreeing to do this again, but as I looked down at the crisp twenty-dollar bills scattered beside me, I wondered if I would even bother to say no. Whatever reservations I had held about going through with it this morning were beginning to fade into the background.

Into the noise of the traffic outside my little window.

I thought about how much further ahead I might be able to get if I did this a few more times.

Just enough to pay some of the bills and maybe even save some until I finished school.

My welfare worker had talked to me about applying for college.

She thought I was smart enough to get accepted into one of the schools here.

She even wanted me to apply to university, but either option meant I had to upgrade quite a few of my high school courses, which I was doing now.

I didn't know how I was supposed to keep going to school and float some kind of part-time job.

I had been given a new worker recently, and she wasn't as easy on me as Gwen was.

She had warned me that if I did manage to get some type of job in the evenings, whatever money I earned from that would be deducted from my welfare cheque, dollar for dollar.

I had never been very good at math, but that calculation didn't make sense to me. Either make $547 a month and complete my schooling or make slightly more than that working around my class schedule, not leaving any room to study.

I didn't really understand how this support system worked.

It didn't seem like they really wanted us to get ahead at all.

Just to stay poor.

The workers seemed to forget what it meant to be poor.

Or maybe they had never known.

It wasn't just not having a car or relying on food banks and soup kitchens for meals.

Sometimes it meant living in neighbourhoods that scared me.

Waking up throughout the night because of the sounds of others fighting in the building.

Spending my last few dollars at an internet café to use a computer with an internet connection just to get my homework done.

Sometimes it was washing my clothes in the sink when I couldn't afford two dollars for the washing machine downstairs. And sometimes it was moments like this.

Selling parts of myself to a man I didn't know to pay for the things I couldn't live without.

When I heard the door close behind him, the emptiness around me came flooding back, and I felt her come back to me.

I felt myself return to my body once more.

I pulled a pillow over, placing it on my stomach and hugging it into myself as I pulled my knees closer to my chest.

You're a whore.

Her words pressed into me like knives.

I felt my body begin to shake again as the tears made their way to my eyes.

You're a whore, she seethed again, waiting for me to respond, to acknowledge her rage.

I carefully wiped a tear from my cheek and stared down again at the money strewn across the bed.

We needed this, I whispered.

I thought she would have more to say to me that day, but she floated away again. And where do you go when you can't get away from yourself but you can't find yourself either?

That is hell, I think.

This is hell.

every day i find more parts of myself
that i want to hide from you
rip away the pages, cut my hair, change my name
because you look at me like i'm sunshine
because you talk to me like i'm sane
because you laugh with me like i'm funny
because you tell me you love my name
and i wonder if you trace the lines
and read the story
if how you look at me will change

— before

April 1st, 2010

I'm outside my apartment, a little nervous,
I have some CVP interview with welfare in a
couple weeks and I don't know if I should be
concerned. Pray I guess. I slept at ███ last
night, and we spent the day together, which was
fun. I want to give the house a good cleaning
and take care of the little guy. I'm still
pretty anxious about just being anywhere. It's
like this pull inside me that's constantly
telling me to get up and go, and I usually do.
So for right now, I'm gonna wait another
few minutes for s██ go inside, tidy up,
pray, clean outside, and just relax. Maybe I
feel stressed all the time because I never stay
home long enough to actually ~~████~~
remember and DO the things I need to do.
I'll impulsively leave for hours, and when I
get home I'm like shit... NOW I remember.
I'll try not to think too much about the night.

Next to the red brick house that held my tiny apartment was a restaurant.

It was a small, cozy place with maybe six or seven tables, neatly tucked away on our quiet street.

If you walked north up our road, you would eventually get to the busier area of downtown.

And if you walked south you would get to an almost deserted end of the city that was close to the highway and bordering the big Greyhound bus station.

Sometimes when I came home, the owner of the restaurant would be standing out front causally smoking a cigarette and taking a much-needed break from the lunch or dinner time rush.

He would greet me every time with a huge smile, telling me to come by if I wanted some food.

It was the kind of invitation that was given with grace and sympathy, and without requiring money.

He knew I didn't have any, and judging by how sick I looked at that time, he probably assumed I didn't have food either.

As the weeks went by, our casual hellos and goodbyes turned into longer conversations.

I began to meet some of the regular customers who would make the drive from all different parts of the city just to eat there.

I watched the way the owner greeted every single person entering the restaurant as if they were family.

And after a while he began to greet me that way, too, in the early mornings as I sat on the front step of the apartment building or at the end of the night as I made my way home from my three- or four-hour walks.

A few months before I went into the hospital, a new face emerged at the restaurant.

A man, maybe a few years older than me.

A relative of the restaurant owner.

He was the definition of tall, dark and handsome.

The kind of person that you meet who you expect to be suddenly nervous around, but to my surprise it was just the opposite.

His uncle introduced us one fall afternoon, and in that moment I knew I had nothing to be nervous about.

It obviously ran in their family to be welcoming and warm towards new people.

After a few weeks, he began to come outside the restaurant more often, tapping on my apartment window with offerings of freshly made food.

I would often come outside and we would sit on the front step, sometimes for hours, chain-smoking and talking about everything.

I slowly began to confide in him about how my life had unfolded recently.

It felt good to talk to someone like this.

We would chain-smoke cigarettes and I would talk to him about what I wanted in life, what had gone wrong, the boys I liked that week or the course I was taking in school.

And through all my ranting, he would sit, listening intently, never interrupting me or brushing off anything I had said, even it if sounded crazy.

It felt good to be heard.

I didn't have to say too much about the eating, as it was obvious by my appearance that I probably wasn't consuming the generous plates he would give me.

Maybe he knew that.

Maybe that's why he kept doing it.

On one particular night, I was talking to him about all the things I wanted to change.

He took a long drag off his cigarette and looked out into the empty street in front of us before saying something that would change how I thought about life.

The life I was living with myself.

"You know… you gotta learn how to be friends with yourself."

Over the years, I had heard things like this before.

In the treatment centres or the AA meetings, countless anecdotes about loving yourself, but there was something about the way he said it, the day, the time, the place, or maybe it was just the fact that I was really hearing him.

It's funny how sometimes we can hear familiar words come at an unfamiliar time, and suddenly it connects.

"This life is just gonna keep going, you know? I know you got friends and meetings and hey you even have us right now," he smiled, nodding towards the restaurant, "and you'll meet a lot of good people in your life, but there's nobody who's gonna have your back like you will…. You're gonna wake up and go to bed with yourself every day."

I took a deep breath in and leaned into the hard concrete edge behind me.

I remember a long time ago when Nina had told me I should take myself on dates. I had cringed at the thought of sitting alone in a movie theatre or taking myself out for coffee.

In that moment, I wondered if I was friends with myself.

I wondered what that even meant.

I knew I lived in my body... I spent the most amount of time with myself because, after all, I can't get away.

But I wondered if all the years I had spent trying to get away... maybe that stopped me from really finding out who I was.

I knew how I liked my coffee because I copied other people's orders.

I picked my clothes out in the morning, giving more time and attention to pieces that someone else had told me they liked.

I used to add salt to a pot of boiling water only because I saw my mother do it once.

I even used to tell people I hated cheese because I heard a really pretty girl say it once.

Who hates cheese?

But besides these little examples I was thinking of, I could tell the real reason he said that was because it was obvious by the way I looked that I wasn't taking care of myself.

That I may, in fact, not be friends with myself.

How casually I had learned to betray my own body, my own mind.

How heavy the armour I wore was beginning to feel.

We talked about a lot of other things that night, sitting on the front steps, chain-smoking cigarettes and laughing loudly into the half-deserted street.

And over many weeks and months, he became my safe place for just a little while.

Someone who didn't look at me like I was sick.

Someone who went out of their way to make me smile or make me laugh. Someone who listened.

Someone who saw life in me that I wasn't even sure was there.

I hope one day you read this, even if it's just this part.

I never really got to say thank you... so, thank you.

For turning a light on in such a dark time.

May 11th, 2010
I finally got an agenda so I won't
have to bore you with my to do lists.
Oh my- guess what? Okay I'll tell you...
Dad called me last night to see how
my first day went! I couldn't even
believe it, it was awesome.
Last night

May 12th, 2010
School is going well - it's really busy,
but I love it so far. I'm at Home.
I feel pretty depressed right now.
I ate a lot and I made Rules that
I wouldn't, I don't know what to do.
Lets weigh in.

May 27th, 2010

There's a part of me that can't stop thinking about it. I fantasize about running into him somewhere and hurting him so violently. Just to cause him a small percentage of pain compared to that which he inflicted on me. I just don't want him to spend his days thinking it was okay. I want to scar him so he always remembers. I've never wanted to hurt someone like this before. It's not fair.

Anyways - on a positive note, I fell asleep last night around 8:30pm, and woke up once at one thirty; then slept till 6:30am. I feel totally refreshed and ready to go. I ate ▮▮▮ pizza last night, and on top of that, did groceries which was intense. I started reading this book (memoir) about a girl with anorexia, and I have to admit, her and I are quite alike. She's trying to explain how she's not sick, and I totally get it! Why are we all so blind?

"How you doing, Kid?"

The voice was familiar, comforting.

I spun around to see Roger, beaming as he always did when he greeted me here.

I was finally starting to become a regular at this meeting.

I liked that people recognized me now and reached out to hug me or shake my hand when I came in.

There was something nice about someone being happy to see me despite how deeply uncomfortable I felt with myself.

"I'm okay," I smiled.

"Okay is good," he said, pulling a chair over to me.

I sat down beside him, letting the weight of my constantly oversized bag slump to the floor.

I hadn't realized just how tired I was.

The journey from downtown to this little church in the west end of the city was long and difficult in the thick winter snow.

"I heard from Grace that you do quite a good job with cleaning?"

I looked out across the room and spotted Grace, who was talking happily with someone. She and I were starting to become quite good friends.

Despite our obvious age difference, we had bonded more recently in our long chats before and after these meetings.

She had invited me over to her house a few days before, offering me a cash job to help her with some housework.

When I arrived her house, I realized she probably didn't actually need any help cleaning, but I think she knew that I needed help living, and maybe that was her way of offering me a hand without taking an ounce of my pride with it.

"Yeah, I did some work there recently," I said, looking back to Roger.

"Well, Pam and I could really use a hand at our place if you're interested. You just tell me your price and I can pick you up and drop you off after."

Say yes.

"I think…. Yeah…. I think that would work," I said, as some part of me began to relax.

You won't have to see Pablo anymore.

I thought about the jobs I had applied for that week, none of which seemed to fit around my school schedule.

Maybe this would be okay.

I was good at cleaning.

My mother had certainly taught me well in my younger years.

And I had made enough money with Pablo over the last few months that I was even able to get myself on a new phone plan, one where the minutes didn't run out.

I had come to hate seeing his name pop up on the screen.

"How are your classes going?" Roger asked, pulling me away from my deeper thoughts.

"I think I'm almost done… just a couple more math courses and one English and then… then I can apply to college…" I trailed off for a moment, suddenly excited at the thought of almost being finished.

It was closer than I had thought.

Three more courses.

"That's great, Kiddo!" Roger boomed excitedly, patting me on the back.

I caught myself smiling.

A big, effortless smile.

My future had often felt like it was a bit out of reach.

Like a boat you see floating off in the distance that looks small and flimsy, but the closer it gets to you, the bigger it becomes. You can start to make out its curves and crevices, and you realize it's actually not flimsy at all.

It's made of something much stronger.

The people I met in those meetings, those rooms, often reminded me how close that future actually was.

And although I wouldn't stay there forever, six years was a long time.

It was a long time of learning and listening and being allowed to grow.

Being in a space where I could learn about what it means to build friendships, what it means to be honest, and to have people get to know me while I was still in the process of getting to know myself.

I grew up in those rooms.

It was letting go and holding on.

It was breaking myself down into a million pieces and having someone like Roger or Grace sit next to me and not look at me like I was crazy.

Or like I was broken, but instead like I was a girl.

A human.

And I would find my way.

And I think that is what led me home in the end.

Having people look at me and know that I wasn't lost.

I was just going home.

I don't want to scare you; I just want you to consider that this whole thing may be bigger that you. I no you don't mean to hurt these people. I wish I could single-handily stop all of this, but I can't + I'm not meant to. Focus now. keep your eyes on the action you can take. there is always hope.

(6) came to ██████ celebration.

God, thank you. ██████████ back. I'm @ ██████ 43 years @ Pinecrest. I just ate a timbit.

August 12th, 2010
Progress:
(1) readings
(2) cleaned mum + Dads
(3) kept myself composed when I thought ████████ was there.
(4) went to Dr ██████████

I'm just tipping a ██████████ yesterday morning I collapsed right in front of the church. that was embarressing. ██████████ Anyways I went + did the work for and that went alright. After I went to see ██████ + talked to Her about things. Then ██████ picked me up and dropped me @

Sept 29th, 2010
Well, Bagley, after dentist: I have
holes in my teeth from the purging,
mild acid decay, 1 visible cavity, + smoke
stains. But guess what? I don't care
cuz Dad's going to treatment.
I got an email from him today and
he said he's realized he's got a drinking problem + he's going to Bellwood
next week. I started crying, I am so
happy for him. whatever happens, I am
very proud of him.

October 5th, 2010

Day ①

Guess where I am? I checked into the general just before 11am. ███████████ brought me here. At present moment: I feel disgusting, confused, shell-shocked. I miss ██████ terribly but I'm trying not to think about it. I've cried a couple times and my stomach is really full so its pretty uncomfortable.

The girls here are all really nice. We share the floor ≥ the psyche patients so its an interesting mix of individuals. I just wanna wear sweaters and sweatpants and ignore everyone healthy I know. I still feel like I'm on a weekend trip or something; even though it's Tuesday. I'm waiting for ██████ right now she's supposed to come visit @ 7pm. There's so much free time here, I'm losing my shit.

"You'll need to wear this," the nurse said, handing me a bracelet with a small, white, oddly-shaped device attached to it.

At first, I thought it was a watch of some kind, but as I surveyed the little circular contraption attached to it, I noticed it lacked a minute or second hand or digital display.

"It's a tracking device. The ones for you girls will be turned off. But you'll need to wear it along with everyone else on the floor."

Seems a little extreme.

"We're trying out a new system to see if we can contain the runners," the nurse laughed, motioning down the hall where Elizabeth was slowly making her way towards us.

Her daily attempt to leave the unit, however, by the time she got halfway up the hallway she would usually forget where she was going.

Elizabeth was a small, frail woman who looked to be about a hundred or so.

Come to think of it, I'm not sure if I ever knew her real name. She would wander into various rooms throughout the day, grinning from ear to ear and introducing herself differently each time, her bright blue eyes shining behind a pair of the largest framed glasses I had ever seen.

She would tell me about how she used to be a beauty queen, and about how she once won an award for her paintings. And of course, she would often tell all of us about an upcoming tea party she was having later that day with the queen of England. The passion behind her words would have made some of her stories quite convincing if we weren't living in the psych ward. One of the rules here was that our doors had to stay open at all times.

This made Elizabeth's daily adventures all the more interesting... and consistent.

When I first arrived here, one of the nurses told me that the funding had been cut for the eating disorders program, which meant that instead of having our own separate unit, the program was moved into the general psychiatric ward.

There were five or six of us in the eating disorders section at any given time, and we were placed in three rooms along the east side of the unit.

A feeble attempt to keep us somewhat segregated from the general ward population.

I didn't mind interacting with the rest of the patients here.

To be honest, the way my mind had been working over the last little while, maybe the west wall was exactly where I needed to be.

"Ten minutes until breakfast," the nurse said suddenly, as she looked up from her watch.

"Are you sitting with us today?" I asked.

"I sure am, Hunnie," she smiled, pulling a stack of papers towards her from the desk below. "Let me get these chart notes done and I'll be right down."

Part of the rules for us on the ward was that we had to eat our meals together, supervised by one of the nurses.

The first week of this was the hardest, and the other girls warned me that it would be. I remember thinking to myself how fuckin stupid this was that we had to sit together for an hour, each of us carefully picking at our trays.

If the bulimia doesn't make you puke, the hospital food will.

She had a point. But after not bothering to plug my fridge in for six months before coming here, let alone fill it with food, I didn't feel this was the time or place to complain.

I walked down the hallway along the west wall that led towards our dining room. As I walked, I heard the familiar rattle of the food carts being wheeled off the elevator.

A quiet patter of footsteps could be heard coming from Antonio's room.

The feeble looking Italian man appeared in his doorway, as he always did at meal times, but he only spoke when he heard the carts. And he only said one word.

"Policia!"

"Good morning, Antonio," I smiled.

As I passed his room, he looked to me, the perpetual look of confusion in his eyes that hadn't seemed to change since my first day here. He raised his arms into the air and screamed again.

"Policia!"

An orderly passed by me in the hall on his way to greet him.

"No police my friend, just breakfast."

I made my way into the little dining room that we shared three times a day.

Jess was already in there setting up the stereo with her choice of music.

That was one of the other things we could do here.

Pick songs to listen to as we all moaned over the pre-packaged cheese slices and lumpy rice cereal.

The Glee soundtrack... again.

Quiet, I thought back to myself.

This was the only time I ever really saw Jess smile, when we listened to these ridiculous musical numbers with her.

And looking back now, I'm glad we did.

I'm glad we had those moments together.

On one fall evening a couple years from now, Jess's tired and gentle heart would stop beating in her sleep.

A final white flag being waved within this horrendous battle.

But for now, for today... we would eat bagels, and between the tears we would sing her favourite songs at the top of our lungs.

The act of sitting and eating together was something most of panicked over, but it also allowed us, in that moment, to really see each other.

To cry or laugh or dance ridiculously.

To hold each other when the anxiety was overtaking us or to wipe each other's tears as the empty trays were taken away, our bodies reeling in panic with the knowledge that we were being fed.

And I wondered sometimes what it really was we were so distraught about.

The feeling of being fed, being full, was obviously the one thing we were each trying to avoid.

The emptiness inside of us had its own room within our bodies.

Its own space to shift and sway and occupy, and within it,
although there was nothing, in reality, it was everything.

All our sadness, our lost dreams, our forgotten years.

All our misplaced expectations.

All floating inside that little space.

In the emptiness.

To fill it physically somehow also began to fill it
metaphorically... but with what? The doctors told us it was for
our own good.

For our health.

For our bodies to begin to work again, our hair to grow back,
our fingers and toes to feel the warmth of our blood once more.

For our heartbeats to regulate, our organs to function, our
minds to come alive. But I can tell you, that is not how it feels at
first.

It feels like terror.

It feels like we are somehow betraying our own minds.

That we are taking away the very thing that was allowing us to
hold on.

So how do you hold on?

When the only coping skill you have left is being torn from you.

When the sudden realization takes hold that you cannot live like
this forever, or even for now.

How do you hold on?

You let go.

i know they are coming for you
in waves
and then all at once
and how i've fought just to keep you
behind you, beneath you
just a little
would be just enough
so tell me dear one
what can i become
while your nails sink deep in my skin?
i could burn all the stories
curse the floorboards below me
but you keep coming back from the dead

— *4 north*

"What do you think brought you here?"

The psychiatrist visited our floor sometimes.

Not often enough to really form any kind of relationship, but often enough to write down in some little chart book that she was there.

It was one of the only times that we had scheduled programming.

The very real cost of the program being underfunded.

Most of us would spend our days reading, writing or wandering the hospital.

One of the only things now that set us apart from the other ward patients was that after the first little while, we would earn our pass to be able to come and go from the unit.

This morning it was my turn to meet with the group psychiatrist.

She was a tall and broad woman who spoke in a slow and painfully monotone voice.

She seemed to carry a constant look of boredom.

I often wondered if she disliked her job or perhaps had been working here for so long that she no longer had the ability to be surprised or particularly enthralled with anything we would say.

Or maybe I had already made up my mind that I wouldn't tell her a thing.

Maybe.

We had two types of sessions with her.

One was group therapy where we would sit together in the little dining room, and we would go around in a circle, taking turns being asked about our lives.

And the other kind was this.

Individual sessions.

It had been quite a while since I had sat alone with a psychiatrist or therapist.

I thought back to my last session so many seasons ago.

My father's insurance had covered five sessions for the year, which had quickly been used up.

I remember the doctor had suggested I continue to meet with her then and even offered to lower her rate to $150 per hour. I had laughed to myself on the bus ride home that day, thinking about the thirty-six dollars left in my bank account and how that needed to last me another two weeks.

Guess we might not see her again.

I guess not.

One of the things about being in the hospital was that we didn't need to pay for these meetings with the ward psychiatrist.

I wondered if that was part of the reason we had so few sessions.

I didn't feel so bad about not being able to afford my own therapy, seeing as how our hospital couldn't seem to afford it either.

I leaned back in the cold metal armchair and met the doctor's gaze, thinking about her opening question.

"I couldn't really function anymore, I guess," I answered honestly.

I thought about my tiny apartment with the heavy blue door and how I had gotten a notice several months before that the electricity was going to be cut off.

I had looked around the apartment wondering what I could possibly turn off to try and save money.

I didn't have the money to pay the bill and was overwhelmed with anxiety at the thought of having to ask my parents for it. Something I had prided myself on not doing.

Ever.

I had decided in that moment that since the fridge wasn't being put to use, I was better off unplugging it along with the stove and the untouched microwave.

I had used every bit of strength I had to turn the heavy yellow refrigerator around so that its door faced the wall.

Some kind of hallowed act of defiance against my starving body.

And I remembered how proud of myself I had been for being able to accomplish that.

Wow.... You really are a bit fucked.

Shut up.

Although the doctor's lack of attention created a distance between us, my inability to trust her didn't particularly stop me from telling the truth.

Not today.

I was tired, after all, and I think the more tired you are of your life the more honest you will be about it.

"Have you ever been admitted to hospital before?" she asked quietly.

Not for this.

I had been looking at my hands when she asked me this, and as I heard her words, my eyes glanced over to the thick white scar on my right wrist.

I wondered how so much time had already passed since that happened.

Images of that night swiftly shot through my mind, and I thought about Dillon.

He had left town shortly after that night.

I didn't blame him, truly.

Our relationship was never the same after it happened.

A mix of misplaced responsibility and fear seemed to haunt him, and I couldn't tell anymore if he was scared of me or scared for me.

Maybe both.

Maybe both.

It hurt me to think that after all we had been through, our demons, however boldly they had strung us together, had pulled us apart just as quickly.

"I tried to kill myself last year," I said, wondering if hearing myself say that out loud would evoke some kind of emotion in me.

It didn't.

On any of the rare occasions where I said something to a listening ear about some of things I had experienced, the harder things, I would often sit and wait for my body to respond.

For my mind to connect or for the tears to begin to flow.

Most of the time I would be met with the same numb, melancholy response.

My body would feel frozen and my mind would simply shut down.

No thoughts or feelings would surface, but instead, a stillness would emerge. Much like the night it happened.

It was almost as if every bone, every cell within me, knew that if I truly connected to those feelings, to that pain, I would come undone.

Fall apart.

And when you weigh ninety-two pounds and your hair is falling out, there doesn't seem anywhere else to fall to.

"Can you tell me about what happened?"

No.

"I uh…. I was just having a hard time," I said, looking up at the doctor, whose pen was writing frantically on the notepad in front of her.

You were having a hard time?

You slit your wrist.

I think that's a little more than a hard time.

"And what do you think was contributing to that?" she asked, not taking her eyes from the page in front of her.

Everything.

I thought back to that night, and not just that night, but the years before, the years after, everything that had happened.

I thought about high school and the people I had known and the places I had run from.

I thought about the treatment centres and the shelter.

I thought about how distant I was from my family.

And I thought about my little apartment with the heavy blue door.

And I thought about that night, with the blood on the floor and the paramedics, and the doctor at the hospital peering over me as he injected lidocaine into my wound while scolding me for my desperate attempt at relief.

You can't even fuckin kill yourself right.

But I didn't say any of this to the doctor.

In that moment it felt utterly useless to tell her these things.

After today, I would not see her again.

We both knew this.

I did not trust her enough to tell her my secrets.

And deep down, I did not trust myself enough to be able to deal with them either.

So, I said what I felt.

Nothing.

Nothing.

October 14th, 2010   Day ⑩
Bah! I got off-ward unaccompanied,
and day passes for the weekend!
I'm having an aleight day. We're in
talk group eight days to now. I don't
believe in psychotherapy but I am
trying to keep an open... ear.
I read the poem in community, and I really
liked it when I read it out loud.
I think I really need to get a start on
that Dr. Paul ⊖ book. I just about went
to 10 with the shrink. It just frustrates
me. And can I tell you something?
✓ but don't tell anyone. ✓ Nevermind. I
don't wanna talk shit about people, it's
not nice. Lets just leave it at that.
MAN, either I have a real issue ⊖ people
being emotional or - NO - thats not true.
When my friends are upset + need my
help I'm there for them, and if they
don't want my help I don't push it.
Being in this therapy; and not just
talk group, but the general - I get
angry when I hear people talking

you promised me a home
a very very long time ago
and i slowed my breathing
and i held my tongue
because i wanted to go there
i wanted to see what that would feel like
but the farther i walked
became the faster i ran
as i realized this road led to nowhere
and the river flows empty
while the sun beats relentlessly
so when the crows swoop down for me
bring me home

— home

The elevator doors opened, and I pushed myself within the crowd of people merging towards them.

It was always busy like this at the end of the day.

Swarms of hospital staff from various departments either beginning or ending their shifts.

Friends and family members coming to visit loved ones, and patients, like myself, navigating the various floors and hallways that seemed to all blend into each other.

I pressed myself into the small elevator, moving myself as far back as I could to allow the others more room to get on.

As I leaned into the small back corner, my arm brushed up against someone, as it does in tight spaces like this.

I looked over at the girl standing beside me to find her looking at me carefully, and as our eyes met, she smiled.

I recognized her.

"Hey," she said quietly, acknowledging that she also remembered me from somewhere.

High school.

She was nice.

The memories began to connect instantly as I realized where I had seen her before.

She lived a few streets away from my parents' house, and we had taken the same bus to school while I was living there.

She was a tall, beautiful girl.

Her pale complexion brought alive by her boldly cut auburn hair and piercing green eyes.

I hadn't spoken to her much during our time in high school, but she had always stood out to me.

She was quiet and had a simpleness about her that held an air of mystery.

The kind of person who may not speak very often, but you can tell by the way they look at people that they think deeply.

About everything.

"It's nice to see you," I said quietly, smiling back.

"What are you doing here?" she asked curiously.

I glanced down at her arm, which was holding a textbook.

I tried to make out the title, something about psychology fundamentals.

She's a student.

I looked up at her quickly to see her surveying the thick white bracelet around my wrist, her question being answered.

"I'm staying here for a while," I said, feeling a sudden flood of stupidity, insecurity.

Of course she was a student.

That's what you do after high school, after all.

You go to college and try to carry on with the normal trajectory of life.

The one that is socially acceptable and expected.

People move on with their lives.

"Oh, Hunnie…." Her voice filled with sympathy. "What happened?"

A million thoughts entered my mind, and I thought about the way these last few years had unfolded.

The decisions I had made.

And the ones that had been made for me.

It was far too long of an answer to give.

Part of me wanted to tell her everything.

Every single thing.

Every fuckin detail.

Even if she didn't want to listen, just to have someone from back then, from back there, hear the whole story.

I felt constantly misunderstood back then, but not in a general way, just in one very specific way.

One very specific story.

That I was never able to tell.

I wanted to take this moment with someone who knew me then but didn't know me now and make them understand what happened.

But that's not what you do in situations like this.

And although she was a sweet girl, she was not the one I was angry with.

I knew that.

As I looked at her and her textbook, I was reminded in such a short encounter how many years I had lost to this…. This… prison.

It was a lot.

I looked down at my bracelet, feeling the elevator pulse and sway at its next stop.

The fourth floor.

My floor.

"It's a long story," I said, smiling awkwardly and readying myself for the elevator doors to open.

It seemed I was the only one getting off here.

"Take care of yourself, Hun," she said softly.

I'm trying.

the rain never cares who it touches
falling confidently to the earth
dripping down into your bones
and mine
unapologetically
and as these wounds open
one by one
they fall off of my tongue
just like that rain
never caring who it touches
dripping down into your bones
and mine

— clean

A few times a day on the ward we would hear the hospital intercom system being turned on, and a voice would boom through the speakers around us, calling a "code white." Almost immediately, it would be followed by the sound of several heavy-footed security guards, followed by nurses or doctors, running down one end of the hallway or the other, responding to whichever patient was in distress. After a few weeks of this, it became quite a regular part of our day.

And you would occasionally hear the noises, usually followed by a struggle with security, and then whichever patient was acting up wasn't seen for a while on account of their medically-induced nap.

As much as I tried to act like these scenes didn't bother me, it is something that I could never quite become accustomed to.

The sounds of another human being moaning in the agony that haunts them. Hearing them cry out while grown men forcefully restrained them and the medical staff offer their only viable solution to the chaos.

I wondered if anyone ever asked them about their lives.

Although I knew they probably did.

But I wondered if anyone was ever listening.

One of the nurses who sat with us during lunch sometimes called it a dissociative episode.

I had heard of this happening to people, but the first time I ever saw it was watching Isabelle.

Isabelle was one of the first girls from our program I met when I arrived here.

She was a wickedly bright girl, about two or three years older than me.

One morning, I had passed by her room to see her curled up on her old white hospital bed reading a Russian dictionary.

She could speak three languages fluently and was brushing up on a fourth just for fun.

I wondered how on earth she managed to fit all of that knowledge inside of her. She was one of the smartest people I had ever met, and yet with that was also the knowledge that she was struggling deeply with the same problems I was. University degrees and healthy trust funds won't save you from the darkness of your own mind.

One afternoon, the group of us were sitting in the dining area after lunch.

We were talking and joking amongst each other, something we had started doing more often.

The meal times were slowly starting to become a highlight of our time together.

I don't remember exactly what we had been talking about when I noticed that Isabelle no longer seemed to be present in our conversation.

Her eyes were transfixed on the table in front of us as she pressed her hands on either side of her empty meal tray.

She began to shake.

I knew her eyes were not taking in our surroundings anymore, and her ears were no longer hearing our voices.

Whatever images were presenting themselves were showing up as some kind of historical movie reel… and the movie was becoming real to her.

"Stop!" she yelled suddenly, not moving her eyes from the table.

A few of the other girls jumped in surprise as the room went silent, everyone watching Isabelle's frightened face as she pushed herself away from the table, her entire body shaking violently.

"NO!" Isabelle screamed as she threw herself backwards, sliding from her chair, pushing herself against the pale cement wall.

The final light her eyes vanished completely as her mind detached from where she was.

I looked over to the nurse sitting with us, and she shot up, quickly making her way around the table to where Isabelle was perched on the floor.

"Hunnie, look at me," she said, bending down slowly, trying to connect.

"You're safe, you're at the hospital, look at—"

"DON'T TOUCH ME!"

Isabelle pushed herself away from the approaching nurse as quickly as she could, towards the door, tears and terror now flowing from her eyes.

The nurse stood up and circled the table again so she could reach a telephone that was mounted to the other wall. She quickly picked up the receiver.

"Call a code white, get some bodies down here," she said calmly, keeping her eyes on Isabelle.

"STOP!" she screamed again to nothing and no one, pushing a chair towards the table.

"Izz," I looked over at Jess, who was slowly pushing herself away from the table, trying to find a way to go to her.

To gain enough of her attention to peel her away from whatever memory was consuming her.

"It's okay, Izz, you're here with us."

Her attempt went unnoticed by Isabelle, who then launched herself towards the open dining room door and down the hallway.

"You girls stay right here," the nurse said to us before stepping out into the hallway and shutting the door behind her.

The room was silent once more as we sat, looking at the table in front of us, listening to Isabelle's heartbreaking cries for help from the hallway as the heavy-footed security guards made their way to her.

I looked over to Jess who was sitting beside me, an emptiness in her eyes as she began to cry.

I was glad that there were no rules here about keeping our distance from each other.

I reached out and took her hand in mine, which she gripped tightly.

We sat together like that for a long time.

I wondered what the point of all this was.

What sense of direction I could derive from it.

It overwhelmed me greatly to think that at only twenty years old I had somehow managed to travel through three treatment centres, a shelter and now a hospital.

I wondered if things ever really would get better.

Or would I be sifting through the cracks of life, forever haunted by the past I couldn't change and the future I couldn't quite seem to grasp.

You are doing better than you think you are.

I'm not so sure, I thought to myself.

Can't I just fast forward to the part where all of this is over?

The part where I wake up and the bricks across my chest are gone.

The part where I open my eyes to find that I'm in a place that's safe and warm and mine.

The part where I pour myself a cup of coffee in the early morning sunshine, and maybe I'm sitting next to someone I love, having breakfast and talking about our plans for the day.

Maybe I'd have a dog to walk or a cat to feed or even children to care for.

I thought about what it would be like to have kids.

To pack their bags for school, brush their hair, tell them silly jokes and put bandages on little scrapes.

Or had I lost that chance now?

One of doctors here told me weeks ago that kids might not be an option. Something about how eating disorders can affect fertility.

I had stopped listening as I heard those first few words... "You might not be able to."

Don't say that, I had thought.

Don't tell me this is permanent.

That the things I've done, the way that I've lived, will somehow be marked in me forever.

And although that conversation came with so much uncertainty, it was also a moment when I realized I was thinking about the future.

My future.

And good or bad, there was a small part of me that was becoming curious about it. A part of me that wanted to see what would happen, what could happen.

And maybe, just maybe, if I hold on through all of this and was willing to do some things I am uncertain about, like the simpleness of feeding myself, just maybe my tomorrows will be okay. But even more, maybe I'll be able to handle whatever those tomorrows will look like.

And as I sat in that dining room holding Jess's hand as we cried quietly together, I wondered if, in fact, this was the very purpose of all of this mess.

To sit with another human being and just be there.

To offer comfort and some kind of understanding.

Care for each other… and maybe it will teach you how to care for yourself.

the water is cold and ever deep
but you, my love
know how to swim
and the mountain is tall
reaching far past the trees
but you, my dear
know how to climb
and though the memories are alive
reaching down to your bones
you, my love
know how to dream
and while the crows dive deep
to pick your pieces from the shore
you, my one
will learn to fly

— speak

November 1st, 2010 DAY (28)

Good afternoon..

Progress so far.....

① Spoke in group about how I'm really feeling - allowed myself to cry.

② compensated for going to this

③ Got a double double coffee

November 2nd, 2010 DAY (29)

Hello hello!!

It's a day - we are having a day! Lots of progress so far:

① gained ▓▓▓▓ kilo's, hit BMI of ▓▓▓▓,

② started writing back to Dad

③ ~~bought~~ bought myself a card

④ didn't change my outfit

⑤ shared in community about an issue I've kept to under wraps in previous treatments. I received a lot of support from the group.

i try to hold you as you have with me
delicate knives and brutal beginnings
how heavy is the weight of all of this?
all of these bricks
all of this armour
i wonder what would happen if i took it off
how many times have i stripped myself of clothing
only to be covered in steel?

— and I don't know you anymore

I wandered down the hallway on the west wall, making my way towards my room.

I spotted Elizabeth at the end of the hall, shuffling herself into someone's room, her big, bright and perpetually confused smile beaming across her face.

She had probably already stopped into my room by this point, I guessed as I pushed open the door. My roommate Farrah was sitting at the end of her bed hunched over a large notebook, writing.

Farrah was one of the sweetest people I had ever met.

Her intense anxiety had caused a host of different peculiar habits, including picking her hair out and writing pages upon pages of notes in the smallest font possible.

I would lay on my bed sometimes, watching her discard an entire page of notes, cursing herself for making a single spelling mistake.

When she would realize I was looking at her, she would begin apologizing profusely, her words becoming scattered as her stutter began to interrupt her train of thought.

"It's okay," I would say quietly, hoping she would feel comfortable enough with me to settle.

And eventually she did.

After a couple of weeks here, Farrah began to tell me about what her anxiety felt like.

How she would punish herself for eating by taking pieces of her hair out, or spend hours writing, carefully making sure the curve of every letter was positioned just right.

Sometimes we would share stories of the crazy things we had done to avoid eating or of how we would exercise for hours on end in order to avoid the guilt that came with consuming an apple or of giving into our bodies' demand for a complete binge. We talked about how out of control we felt when we would eat or how we avoided any kind of events with friends or family, knowing the plates of food would be too much to handle.

I learned more talking to Farrah in those weeks than I had in any of the therapy sessions I had been to so far.

Watching her frantically scrubbing her shoes, which were only worn inside the hospital halls, made me realize this had nothing to do with eating.

That the reasons we were here, and the reasons we were starving, were more about trying to gain control of our bodies and our emotions.

If I starve, I don't feel.

My body and my mind will redirect its attention to survival. New, soft hair would grow all over me in an effort to retain heat.

The visions that would flash through my mind were no longer haunting bathroom tiles but dreams of all the food I so desperately wanted to eat.

My racing thoughts would be replaced with a slow, delicate stillness.

A vast emptiness.

And that was what I wanted.

To think of nothing and to ache for no one.

I pushed myself onto my bed that afternoon, wondering what the next few weeks or months here would be like.

I wondered if I would leave here, forever haunted, only to self-destruct once again and be brought right back.

That seemed to be the story of so many people on our unit.

Why couldn't I get better?

Why couldn't I just let go of the fuckin memories and come up for air?

Why couldn't I be normal?

You are normal.

This isn't normal, I shot back at myself.

How many years have I lost to this... this sickness?

I can't move on.

Yes, you fuckin can.

I sat for a moment, startled with how demanding my inner voice had become.

This same voice, this same part of myself that wanted me to die not so long ago. The same voice that had sat with me, crying into my pillow, screaming at me to throw up the dinner or walk for hours on end to nowhere.

The same voice that demanded I leave home, leave that part of the city.

The same voice I could never quite tell if she was trying to help me or hurt me.

That same voice.

But my voice.

I've been trying to save you.

Had she?

Was every moment leading to this just a vicious battle, fighting with the part of me that wanted to survive?

There is no one here that is going to force you to do this…. To let go…. To live.

You have to do it yourself.

You have to do it yourself.

But I'm scared. I don't know where to start.

So start scared.

Start here.

What happens if I fuck it up?

Then you try again.

Start again.

What if I don't make it?

Oh, but what if you do?

I feel like I don't even know who I am anymore.

So become who you want to be.

Yeah, okay, just fake it? I thought sarcastically.

Just try.

I rolled my eyes, letting out an audible sigh.

Some kumbaya bullshit, I thought.

If you want to stay in here, then just keeping living like you were, she
spat, irritated.

I don't want that, I thought.

And I didn't.

Who would want to live like this?

*You can either be back here in a few years or dead or… doing something
different.*

But what do I do if it's too much… if I get sick again… if none
of this works?

Then I'll stop asking you to try.

But you have to try first.

You have to find out if it's possible.

You can't hide in these places forever.

I reached across the bed to my nightstand and pulled the small coil notebook over, placing it on my lap.

As I opened the beaten pages, I found an empty space and began to write.

But this time, not just about my day.

I began to write about the things I didn't want to write about.

About the things I didn't want to talk about.

All of it.

Slowly and carefully, the tears I had always spent so much time avoiding began to fall, one by one, landing perfectly along the open notebook, a grateful release.

And I wondered if all this was supposed to make me stronger.

That is an interesting sentiment, isn't it?

I had been told, countless times, that old familiar line we are all told in times of great sadness.

What doesn't kill you makes you stronger.

So where is my strength?

It seemed like all I had found over these years was sadness and desperation.

And every time a well-meaning counsellor would tell me about how this pain had added to my character or made me more resilient, I wanted to sew their mouths shut.

It didn't make me stronger.

It made me sad.

It made me empty and nervous and careless.

The tears continued to fall, one by one, two by two.

I used to pride myself on holding all of this in.

I'd say stupid things, like, "I haven't cried in a year."

A signal that to be so disconnected and unfeeling was some kind of badge of strength.

But it never was.

The truth is, I just didn't know how.

How to connect.

How to be honest.

And aren't you tired of this….

This…

prison?

"Yes," I choked, trying to catch my breath.

Trying to remember the last time she had said those words
to me.

The last time I had felt the walls closing in.

So go.

Go where?

Home.

The one that we can build.

The life that we can build.

Her words, my words, wound their way from my head to my
heart as I leaned my head back on the pillow behind me.

The only thing I knew for certain in that moment was that
finally, after all this time, both her and I wanted the same thing.

Both her and I wanted to live.

And I didn't realize how long I had been waiting to hear her say
that.

To tell me that she was ready to go home.

And it suddenly felt like so many years of trying to hold onto
her…. Onto myself… were finally merging.

She finally wanted to live too.

As I watched myself, pen in hand hovering over the page, I heard the echo of the intercom system calling another code white, followed by a rush of heavy footsteps making their way down the hall.

Please.

Can we go home now?

and the thing is
i believe you
after all the ways you hid from me
struggling to breathe
drowning in empty
i would often wonder if i sat quietly
patiently waiting for you to see me
if you would know
that i've seen what you've seen
i've felt those feelings
i believe you

— *east*

"I want to leave," I said firmly, not taking my eyes from the doctor.

He sighed heavily, removing the thinly-framed glasses from his face with one hand as he rubbed his eyes with the other.

I couldn't tell if this was from irritation or contemplation.

"We usually do not let patients go this early…," he said, looking up to meet my gaze.

Fuck.

Keep going. Tell him why.

"I've done what's been asked…. I've gained the weight back…. I can handle myself outside of here."

He looked at me questioningly.

"There isn't enough… stuff… here," I said, gaining more confidence. "We are alone on the ward most of the day… we don't get regular counselling; shit we don't even have anything to do except for walking up and down the hallways. I've done what has been asked…. I need to go home and start living outside of here."

I put down the letter in front of me.

The one I had spent hours writing and re-writing in hopes I would be able to convince the doctor to let me leave.

Let me go home.

These walls had held me in place over the last two months, just as the other centres before them had, but I needed to go home.

I needed to wander down my street and take in the scenery around me.

I needed to go to a grocery store and learn how to navigate a shopping list.

I needed to turn my fridge around and plug it back in.

I needed to go swimming in a pool with Farrah, like I had promised.

I needed to go hug my friends from the restaurant and finally sit down to a meal with them.

I needed to apply to college.

I needed to get out of here.

Deep down in my soul I knew now that I had to do something. Something new.

Something different.

And I needed to do it now.

Before she didn't want to anymore.

I was scared that if I didn't leave now, if I didn't run with the energy she was giving me, I would stay stuck here forever.

The doctor took a long pause before putting his glasses back on and bringing his pen towards the paper in front of him, making some kind of note that I couldn't see.

"Okay," he said flatly, obviously wondering whether this was the correct response.

Okay?

That's it?

My heart began to race with excitement, or anxiety, I couldn't quite tell.

"So... I can go home?" I asked, hesitating to smile.

He looked at me, our eyes connecting boldly, intentionally.

"If you think that we have done all we can for you here... if you think that you can go back...," he sighed, looking down at the papers in front of him and then back up to me again. "Three days."

I leaned back in my seat, my body relaxing, finally.

"Stay for three more days…. It'll give me time to do up your paperwork."

Thank you.

He glanced down at his notes again.

"You know you can come back if you need to…. If it doesn't go well."

"I know," I said quietly. "But I can't stay here forever…. I need to see if I can do this on my own now… out there," I motioned to the window beside us that looked out across the east end of the city.

You can.

I wasn't sure how or why that voice inside of me had gotten so loud over the last few days.

So sure of what we needed to do.

It felt like some kind of panic had instilled itself inside me.

Some kind of energy, some kind of understanding that I was the only person who would be able to do this.

These things.

These little tasks.

I used to feel safe being away at these centres or in the shelter.

And I guess in those moments when you are broken and quiet, it may be the best place to be.

The softest place to land.

But I didn't feel that way anymore.

I was tired of not being seen.

Of not seeing myself.

Something inside of me was beginning to wake up.

Wondering what would happen if I just… tried.

Tried to do something I wasn't sure I could.

Maybe that night in the apartment when I didn't die, maybe that was a chance for me to do this again.

This life.

And maybe these last few years, going through all these facilities, maybe it wasn't all for nothing.

Maybe it was leading me to here, to this moment, the entire time.

And if it really is going to be a struggle anyway, maybe it would be a little less of a struggle if I ate food and went back to school and talked about the things that hurt.

Or maybe didn't talk about the things that hurt.

Sometimes those moments of silence were just as helpful.

And I didn't know the answer.

But for the first time in a long time, I knew what I didn't want.

I didn't want to watch the rest of my life float away.

Looking out a hospital window, watching the leaves stray from the trees.

And maybe there would be days where I would feel like that again.

Where I would cry or bleed and beg for the end all over.

Maybe.

But isn't there just as much of a chance that I would have joy?

That I would learn to know people and let them know me.

That I would smile at simple things, like flowers in a garden or an old song on the radio. And maybe those things aren't so simple after all.

I didn't know what I was doing that day, but I needed to go.

I needed to become.

they say there is no one coming to save you
because they want you to save yourself
but the truth is
there are so many people coming to save you
and you will save them too
in quiet little stories
stolen glances
and clumsy promises
don't ever believe them when they say no one is coming
they are already here

— wings

The door on the back of the bus opened smoothly as I stepped out into the midday sunlight.

The air was crisp and cool, bringing with it the gentle reminder that fall was here.

Change was coming.

As the bus pulled away, I began walking up my old, familiar downtown street.

The one that almost cut through Chinatown.

The one where if you stopped on the corner of Kent and James around this time of day, you would sometimes hear the church bells.

Even if you didn't believe in God, it was still such a beautiful sound to hear.

I pulled my bag over my shoulder again, readjusting its position, readying myself for the long walk back to my apartment.

The one with the heavy blue door.

I still couldn't really believe I was going home.

Those last three days in the hospital seemed to drag on forever.

The farewells were bittersweet.

I was sure Elizabeth would still be looking for me, or maybe she had forgotten I was ever there by now.

The girls seemed to be filled with emotion.

And as they held me, we all made promises to each other that we would see each other later.

On the outside.

A quiet breeze swept itself around me as I carried on down the busy street.

I came upon the front of the little red brick house.

The one with the five apartments inside.

The one with my apartment.

Home.

I hadn't seen it in a little while, and by the way my body relaxed as I looked at it, I knew deep down I must have missed it.

Even that lumpy black futon.

The front of the building was looking cleaner than usual, and someone had even built a little flower-box beside the front door. It was filled with dirt and waiting patiently for seeds.

As I looked to it, I thought about what that man had said at that meeting so long ago.

About planting seeds.

Even the flowers and the trees seemed to understand that growing takes time.

I felt my phone begin to buzz inside my bag.

I sat down on the crumbling concrete steps that led up to the front door, placing my bag down beside me and reaching inside to see who was calling.

As I pulled my phone out and looked at the number displayed, my heart sank as I saw who it was.

Pablo.

Of course.

Don't answer it.

I thought about the money in my bank account.

All seventeen dollars of it.

It wouldn't be enough to get groceries, and I was eating now, so life was about to become a little more expensive.

You can go to the food bank; it opens at noon.

Okay… I thought, looking down at my shoes, which definitely weren't going to get me through the coming winter.

Call Grace.

She said she wanted you to clean for her again when you got out….

I could do that.

I didn't want to see Pablo again, and in that moment that was the only clear thought I had.

The one I needed to listen to.

I opened my phone, searching frantically for Pablo's contact information.

Do it.

Block.

Delete.

As I watched the number disappear, I felt a sudden relief I hadn't expected.

An excitement.

A quiet curiosity.

I had lived without the money from Pablo before, and I could do it again.

Maybe differently this time.

I thought about what the doctor had said just before I left the hospital:

"Reach out if you need help."

And I know he meant to reach out to him if the eating got bad again, but I wondered if I could reach out in different ways now. I wondered what would happen if I answered questions honestly when asked. Like "How are you?" or "Do you need anything?" Grace asked me that every few days, and I always said that I was fine.

Maybe some of them want to help.

I thought about my math teacher at the high school.

The one who was helping me upgrade my classes in preparation for the college application.

I remembered him saying a while ago that there was a counsellor there I could see and that she would help me with bus fare to get around the city a little easier.

And I thought about my brother.

My sweet, gentle brother, who asked constantly if I was okay, if I needed anything.

When he would come to visit me here, he would always offer to take me to lunch, and I would always say no.

He never made me feel bad or awkward about it, but I could tell he wanted to do something.

To help.

I wondered what would happen if I said yes to people when they offered these kinds of things.

Maybe nothing.

But maybe something.

You don't have to do all of this on your own.

I leaned back against the hard concrete step behind me, thinking about what the next few days, weeks and months would look like. I was sure it would be very different.

New.

Kind of like getting to know myself all over again.

And there was something about it that felt odd and uncomfortable, yet hopeful.

I had spent so much time trying to run from everything and anyone that I couldn't make sense of.

Anything that made me feel sad or scared, but maybe some of the things that are good for me also scare me in the beginning.

That's the thing when you run from everything… you don't just miss some of the bad.

You miss it all.

The people who want to love you.

The experiences that are waiting to shape you.

The opportunities that could change you.

And mixed in between all of that will still be pain, setbacks, surely some lonely nights and even lonelier days… but maybe those are the days where I would learn to do things a little differently.

Where I would search for answers.

And isn't that what we are all doing here anyways?

Searching.

Finding meaning among the joy and the pain.

But maybe that's just it.

Maybe there is no deeper meaning in the pain.

Maybe it just hurts.

Maybe its only purpose is to force you to find the joy.

And I wondered what had changed in me.

I think that was it.

I just wanted to start searching for the joy.

on that day I made a promise
that only you and I could hear
that I would follow you
down every street, on every day
and you ran faster
testing my word
wondering what I would say
and every corner you turn
we collide once again
and I'd remind you
I'm going to stay
so run from me darling
far through the hills
and I'll pull you back out from the dark
and if the night holds our secrets
then the day cannot keep them
we can keep coming back to the start

— hills

I closed my eyes for a moment, allowing the darkness to swallow me as I found myself back in that café.

At 1:47 in the morning.

My seventeen-year-old self, shaking on those cold and bloodied tiles.

I looked down at her wondering why I had hated her so much.

All these years spent punishing a younger version of myself, begging for a different ending to the same story.

I knelt down, watching her scared and pale face reaching for answers.

Answers I didn't have back then.

I reached out and took her hand, pulling her to her feet, wrapping my arms around her as she screamed her pain into the empty space surrounding us.

We're going home, I whispered to her.

I pulled her out of that café.

I began to show her how she tried to survive.

Changing the old familiar narrative we had lived with.

I showed her the places we had been and the people who had been there and had tried their best to pull us from this chaos.

And I showed her the apartment and the knife and the exhaustion we lived with each day, scrambling to find answers, to find hope.

I apologized for not taking better care of her.

For forcing her to run from herself.

For every cold disregard of her pain.

And then I showed her the rising.

I showed her turning that old yellow refrigerator around, her hands shaking as she filled it with food for the first time.

I showed her trudging through the snow with her little basket of cleaning supplies, a full month's worth of work ahead.

I showed her hugging her brother and eating dinners with her family again.

I showed her laughing and singing at the top of her lungs with her best friend as they drove through her new neighbourhood.

I showed her going to a concert with her dad, laughing and joking together on the ride to the music hall.

I showed her framing her college diploma.

I showed her sitting with a client, listening to their story of heartbreak that was quite similar to ours. Not taking any notes. Just listening.

I showed her dancing around her apartment in her wedding dress on a sunny fall afternoon.

I showed her the son she had.

I showed her finally getting that job she had been wanting.

I showed her becoming a single mother, reminding her gently that we are not immune to the tides of life, to the pain.

But oh, how we can overcome.

I showed her walking our dog in the early morning sunshine, smiling to her neighbours as they called her by name. They knew her.

I showed her becoming the kind of friend she had wanted.

I showed her becoming the kind of person she could love.

And then I showed her walking into an office that looked quite familiar, saying that she was finally ready to talk about the things that had haunted her.

To heal.

And I showed her herself.

Living... and wanting to live.

I watched her eyes open, illuminated by the life we almost missed.

The one we weren't sure we would get to.

I'm bringing you home.

And we are okay in the end.

And you will be too.

And look at what grows in the space it left behind.

3 a.m. Thoughts

I wondered if I had held onto all of this for long enough now.

For too long.

Pain is a funny thing, isn't it?

It can make you do terrible and beautiful things.

All while convincing you that none of it really means anything anyways.

I wondered when I would have that moment where I would just wake up and be... Different.

Feel different.

Act different.

I had wanted that so much.

To roll over one morning and suddenly realize I was no longer tormented by those things.

Those little memories.

Those massive moments.

I would listen to the things people would say to me.

The advice.

The guidance.

The concern.

I would hang onto those words, wondering if inside of one of those conversations I would suddenly have this great realization.

This powerful moment of healing.

I ached for that.

And now when I look back, I can see that that's what was happening all along, wasn't it?

Only in small and simple moments.

Quiet conversations and difficult decisions.

Or maybe even in the silence.

I've been making my way here the entire time.

In every centre, every room, every paved street, every crumbling sidewalk, I've just been making my way out of the darkness.

Step by step.

So, no, it doesn't just happen all at once.

I didn't wake up one morning and feel free.

Feel healed.

But I did wake up every morning and decide that even when my body ached and my mind screamed at me to give up... I would keep going.

For just a little bit longer.

And maybe you can too.

And maybe I'll meet you one day, wherever you are in your journey.

Whatever dark road or bright street you are travelling down.

Maybe I will see you and you will see me and we will remind each other that we can keep going.

I hope so.

I hope I meet you there.

I believe you.